The appearance of Wordsworth's and Coleridge's *Lyrical Ballads* (1798) and of Wordsworth's preface to the second edition (1800) have generally been regarded as the first major landmark of a new era in English literature. The authors announced a fresh approach to poetry, their purpose being 'to throw over incidents taken from common life a certain colouring of the imagination, whereby ordinary things should be presented in an unusual aspect ...' In these early poems Wordsworth gives us, as Professor Watson expresses it, 'A poetry the texture of which allows no escape'. He stresses the skill with which Wordsworth varies his language according to the character of each poem, and concludes that the language of *Lyrical Ballads* should be seen as a whole: we should beware of regarding the more elevated diction of 'Tintern Abbey' as the true voice of Wordsworth, and of writing off the simpler style of the tales.

The main part of the essay is devoted to *The Prelude*, in which the author finds some important points of resemblance to *Paradise Lost*. Although *The Prelude* is ostensibly an autobiography, it deals with the loss of the paradise of childhood and in some respects raises the long autobiographical poem to the level of epic. The final section considers the sonnets and *The Excursion*, Wordsworth's later and more sombre meditation on the central problems of human life. The essay explains in many contexts, both in Wordsworth's prose and his verse, his fundamental conceptions of the poet as a human being who shares the joys and sorrows of all mankind with a more than common enthusiasm.

The author is Professor of English Literature in the University of Durham. His publications include *Picturesque Landscape and English Romantic Poetry* and *Wordsworth's Vital Soul*, a study of the sacred and the profane in Wordsworth's poetry (1982). He is the editor of a major anthology, *Everyman's Book of Victorian Verse*, of a 'casebook' on Browning and of an edition of Hardy's *The Mayor of Casterbridge* (1983).

¶ WILLIAM WORDSWORTH was born at Cockermouth, Cumberland, on 7 April 1770. He died on 23 April 1850 and is buried in Grasmere Churchyard.

Writers and their Work
A critical and bibliographical series

General Editor
Ian Scott-Kilvert

WORDSWORTH

WORDSWORTH

by

J. R. WATSON

PUBLISHED BY
PROFILE BOOKS LTD
WINDSOR, BERKSHIRE, ENGLAND

First published 1984
Profile Books Ltd.,
Windsor, Berks
© J. R. Watson 1984

Printed in England by
Unwin Brothers Limited,
The Gresham Press, Old Woking, Surrey

ISBN 0 85383 638 8

Printed and bound by CPI Group (UK) Ltd, Croydon, CR0 4YY

CONTENTS

FOR MORRIS AND ESMÉ DODDERIDGE

WILLIAM WORDSWORTH

I. LIFE

In his great autobiographical poem, *The Prelude*, Wordsworth tells the story of his early years; but it is important to remember that the truth was more complex than the poem suggests. *The Prelude*, like all poems, selects its own imaginative material from the experience on which it is based; and many of Wordsworth's poems are founded on his own life and his interpretation of it. To understand his poetry fully, we need to know something of Wordsworth's life, in more detail than we do with other poets whose imaginations are not so intricately connected to their own experience.

William Wordsworth was born at Cockermouth, Cumberland, on 7 April 1770, the second child of John and Ann Wordsworth. John Wordsworth was an attorney, the 'agent' of Sir James Lowther, for whom he acted in legal and political matters. The Wordsworth children were born in a substantial house in Cockermouth, where the family lived until 1778; but in March of that year Ann Wordsworth died, and the family was split up. William's beloved sister Dorothy (born 25 December 1771) was sent to live at Halifax with her mother's cousin, and the boys were sent to school at Hawkshead. Fortunately they were well educated there and well cared for: they lived in a cottage with an old lady named Ann Tyson, who took in school boarders and who seems to have given them the right amount of affection and freedom. The impression conveyed by *The Prelude* is one of extraordinary energy and activity, but also of normality; he played games, both indoor and outdoor, with a natural exuberance and enthusiasm.

On 30 December 1783, when William was thirteen, his father died; years later he remembered the boyish anticipation of going home for the Christmas holidays and the sadness that followed. The house at Cockermouth had to be given up, and from then on the boys spent their holidays either with their uncle at Whitehaven or, more frequently, at Penrith with their maternal grandparents, the Cooksons, and their uncle, Christopher Crackanthorpe Cookson. There the boys were patronized and made to feel dependent, and William was rebellious: it is clear that his childhood was by no means as uniformly happy as *The Prelude* suggests, and it is of Hawkshead and not Penrith that the poet writes when he looks back to the happiness of the early years.

In October 1787, the young Wordsworth left the Lake District for the first time, to become an undergraduate at St. John's College, Cambridge. Although there were other boys from Hawkshead there, and he was in many ways contented, he was also uneasy in his mind and restless; just how restless may be seen from the marvellous fourth book of *The Prelude*, when he describes the joy of returning to Hawkshead for his first summer vacation. The most spectacular evidence of his unease came two years later, in the long vacation of 1790, when he and his friend Robert Jones undertook a strenuous walking tour through France and Switzerland. By then he had given up any intention of getting an honours degree, and his leaving Cambridge at a time when he might have been preparing for examinations was a snub to the academic life. The tour itself, which gave rise to *Descriptive Sketches* and later to the sixth book of *The Prelude*, was one of the great imaginative experiences of Wordsworth's life.

It was followed by an unsettled period: after graduating from Cambridge without honours in January 1791, he lived in London for some months before spending the summer in Wales, revisiting Cambridge, and then leaving for France in November.

His motive for visiting France was probably to learn

the language: the results were very different. First, in a country that was experiencing a revolution he received his early political education, partly from his own observation and partly from his friendship with Michel Beaupuy. Beaupuy was an unusual man, an army officer who was isolated from his fellow officers as a consequence of his revolutionary sympathies. Beaupuy's politics were simple and humane: he was against corruption and poverty, and looked forward to a time when men would live in liberty and brotherhood and the world would be a better place. Second, Wordsworth met Annette Vallon, the daughter of a deceased surgeon of Blois; they became lovers, and she became pregnant.

Thus, in a little over a year, Wordsworth had experienced a remarkable political and sexual awakening. Moreover, it was a time of great events: during his time in France the attack on the Tuileries, the September massacres, the abolition of the monarchy, and the split between the moderate Girondins (some of whom Wordsworth knew) and the Jacobins heralded the trial and execution of the king (21 January 1793) and the Terror. By late December 1792, however, Wordsworth had returned to England; his child, Anne-Caroline, was born and baptized on 15 December.

The following year, 1793, was of considerable importance to Wordsworth in several ways. In the first place, it saw the first publication of any of Wordsworth's poems: *An Evening Walk* and *Descriptive Sketches* appeared on 29 January. Three days later, France declared war on England, and England responded by declaring war on France on 11 February. Wordsworth's response, as he tells us in *The Prelude*, was painfully confused: his natural patriotism conflicted with his hope for the Revolution, and he must also have been disturbed by the separation from Annette and the child. Some of his anger is found in the 'Letter to the Bishop of Llandaff,' an unpublished reply to a sermon on *The Wisdom and Goodness of God in Having Made Both Rich and Poor*: the bishop's appendix to the sermon criticized the French and complacently preferred the British constitution and British justice. Wordsworth's reply demonstrates his impatience with what he called 'the baleful influence of aristocracy and nobility upon human happiness and virtue' (p. 46) and his use of a classic argument for the revolutionary use of force:

> ... a time of revolution is not the season of true Liberty. Alas! the obstinacy & perversion of men is such that she is too often obliged to borrow the very arms of despotism to overthrow him, and in order to reign in peace must establish herself by violence.[1]

(I.33)

The 'Letter' shows clearly Wordsworth's hatred of inherited rank and wealth, of rich clergy, and of the British system of justice (from which he and his brothers and sisters had suffered: after the death of their father, Lowther, now Lord Lonsdale, refused to pay for the work that he had done, and a long and inconclusive lawsuit followed).

It was at this moment that a friend, William Calvert, proposed a tour of the west of England, travelling in a small cart called a 'whiskey': they began on the Isle of Wight, where Wordsworth's anger was probably further inflamed by the sight of the English fleet preparing for war. From there they set out across Salisbury Plain: an accident occurred to the whiskey, and Calvert took the horse, leaving Wordsworth to walk. Salisbury Plain was a desolate part of the country, and his solitude must have seemed to the young poet to be emblematic of his isolation and lonely frustration: he walked northward, past Stonehenge, having frightening visions (*The Prelude*, Book XII, 1805 text) of ancient Britons engaged in savage war and human sacrifice. From there he travelled northwest, to Tintern Abbey and up the Wye valley to his friend Robert Jones in north Wales. The journey was

[1] All prose quotations are from W. J. B. Owen and J. W. Smyser, eds., *The Prose Works of William Wordsworth*, 3 vols. (Oxford, 1974). References are to volume and page numbers.

remembered by him with a peculiar vividness: fifty years later he told Isabella Fenwick that it 'left on my mind imaginative impressions the force of which I have felt to this day' (*Poetical Works*, I.330)[2]. From it came experiences that represent two seminal themes of Wordsworth's poetry: his King Lear-like awareness of the houseless poverty of the outcasts of society, and his vivid appreciation of the beauty of a scene like that a few miles above Tintern Abbey. Meanwhile we may gain some insight into the kind of young man he appeared to be, if we realize that a tinker (who later became Peter Bell in the poem of that name) thought he might be a murderer. He had no doubt been sleeping rough and probably looked unkempt and farouche.

To the following months and years belong a variety of experiences, but none so significant as this remarkable journey on foot. Later in 1793, Wordsworth probably revisited France in secret, supposedly fleeing from Paris when his life was in danger; in 1794 he spent a happy few weeks with his sister Dorothy at Keswick; later in the year he stayed with a friend, Raisley Calvert (brother of William), being his companion during a terminal illness. Calvert died in January 1795, leaving Wordsworth a legacy that enabled him to live independently though simply. He returned to London, where he furthered his acquaintance with the radical political philosopher William Godwin, and in September he accepted the offer of a house in Dorset called Racedown (between Crewkerne and Lyme Regis) from some Bristol friends. There he and Dorothy settled down, and he began to recover from the upheavals of the previous years. He wrote much of the second version of a poem on the Salisbury Plain experience and a verse drama, *The Borderers*; though the main benefit of these years was a steady growth in the belief in his own powers. This was

---

[2] *The Poetical Works of William Wordsworth*, revised edition by E. de Selincourt and H. Darbishire, 5 vols. (Oxford, 1952-1959).

given a powerful boost by the developing acquaintance with Samuel Taylor Coleridge, whom Wordsworth had first met in 1794 and subsequently corresponded with. Coleridge visited Racedown in June 1797, leaping over a gate and bounding across a field in his eagerness to arrive. They read their poems to each other, with mutual delight; by mid-July, after Coleridge had brought William and Dorothy back with him to Nether Stowey (in North Somerset), they had moved into Alfoxden House nearby. There followed a year of buoyant spirits and happy activity, walking, writing, and preparing the *Lyrical Ballads* (1798). The final poem, 'Lines Composed a Few Miles Above Tintern Abbey,' was added in July after a short walking tour with Dorothy, in which they revisited the landscape that Wordsworth had seen in 1793; its confident tone of sustained and assured thankfulness indicates Wordsworth's joy at finding his imagination working at full stretch after the troublesome years that followed his return from France.

Throughout these years, it is difficult to overemphasize the importance of Dorothy Wordsworth's love and care: she continued to have faith in her brother and his poetry, and her vivid appreciation of nature (recorded in her journals) was an inspiration to both Wordsworth and Coleridge. The three left for Germany in September 1798, in the same month that saw the appearance of *Lyrical Ballads*. The plan was to settle near a university town, learn German, and attend lectures. They split up, to avoid speaking English all the time, and the Wordsworths settled in Goslar, during an unusually severe winter: deprived of books and company, William began to write again, composing some of the 'Lucy' poems and the first parts of what was later to be book I of *The Prelude*. They left Goslar in February 1799, and after a short walking tour in Germany returned to England in the spring. In December 1799, they finally came to rest in the Lake District, in the cottage at Grasmere that is now called Dove Cottage. Except for occasional short periods or visits, Wordsworth lived in the Lake District for the rest of his life, at first at Grasmere and (after 1813) at Rydal, the next village.

The first years at Grasmere were years of great happiness, for Wordsworth seems to have felt a very deep sense of homecoming (which is expressed in 'Home at Grasmere,' a poem that remained unpublished at his death). In October 1802 he married Mary Hutchinson, after a brief visit to France to see Annette and the nine-year-old Anne-Caroline; he had known Mary Hutchinson and her family since childhood and stayed with them at their farm at Sockburn-on-Tees after returning from Germany. Meanwhile, Coleridge had settled at Keswick, thirteen miles away, though he was unhappy with his wife and often in poor spirits. He left Keswick for Malta in January 1804, and although the friends met again, there was never the same creative interchange and intimacy that had taken place in 1797–1798. Before leaving, however, Coleridge had introduced Wordsworth to Sir George Beaumont, a wealthy patron and connoisseur, who became a benefactor and friend until his death in 1827: it was to Beaumont that Wordsworth turned for support during the greatest crisis of his adult life, the death of his brother John at sea in February 1805.

The death of John Wordsworth, followed by the growth of the friendship with Sir George and Lady Beaumont, herald the later years of Wordsworth's life. They were, perhaps inevitably, less exciting than before: in 1813 he became Distributor of Stamps for Westmorland, a post that carried with it a commission on the sale of stamps, which amounted to some £400 a year, although clerks and other officials had to be paid out of this. Nevertheless, the post marked a significant change in Wordsworth's status and way of life; similarly, the friendship with Beaumont was with a man who was, unlike Coleridge, conventional and conservative in every way. We can only speculate on the reasons why Wordsworth wrote so little good poetry after 1807; but his increasingly respectable life, and the loss of Coleridge's stimulus, may have been partly responsible.

Apart from some Scottish and Continental tours, Wordsworth remained at Rydal Mount from 1813 to his death on 23 April 1850. In his later years, he was revered and honoured: the University of Durham gave him an honorary degree in 1838, and Oxford followed in 1839; in 1843, on the death of Southey, he became Poet Laureate. His later years were clouded by the protracted illness of his sister, Dorothy, and by the death of his beloved daughter Dora in 1847; but he had the satisfaction of seeing his poems grow in popularity, and his fame spread through the English-speaking world. His faith that his poetry 'must sooner or later work its way into the hearts and minds of the people'[3] had been fully justified.

II. EARLY POEMS

In 1843, Wordsworth said that 'no change has taken place in my manner for the last forty-five years.' This dates Wordsworth's mature style at 1798, with the publication of *Lyrical Ballads*, and suggests that in the earlier poems he had failed to find his own individual voice. At first sight this seems to be the case: *An Evening Walk* and *Descriptive Sketches* (1793) are written in heroic couplets and contain many borrowings and influences from eighteenth-century poets; while another major poem of these years, the Salisbury Plain poem (in two versions), is written in Spenserian stanzas, another popular eighteenth-century form. In other respects, too, they seem conventional, with titles, diction, and description following the eighteenth-century patterns. They were later revised extensively by Wordsworth, and they are best read in the 1793 text, which is printed in many editions. There the reader can see the dominance of the contemporary style:

[3]Mary Moorman, *William Wordsworth: A Biography*, vol. II: *The Later Years 1803–1850* (Oxford, 1965), p. 544.

—Then Quiet led me up the huddling rill,
Bright'ning with water-breaks the sombrous gill;
To where, while thick above the branches close,
In dark-brown bason its wild waves repose,
Inverted shrubs, and moss of darkest green,
Cling from the rocks, with pale wood-weeds between;
Save that, atop, the subtle sunbeams shine,
On wither'd briars that o'er the craggs recline;
Sole light admitted here, a small cascade,
Illumes with sparkling foam the twilight shade.
Beyond, along the visto of the brook,
Where antique roots its bustling path o'erlook,
The eye reposes on a secret bridge
Half grey, half shagg'd with ivy to its ridge.

(An Evening Walk, 71-84)

Here the reader notices immediately the personification of 'Quiet,' the use of words like 'sombrous,' 'illumes,' and 'visto,' the use of inversion, with a latinate postponement of the main verb, and the use of a Latin participial construction, 'Sole light admitted here,' to make an adjectival phrase. All these disappear in later versions, which suggests that Wordsworth himself came to regard them as blemishes on the poem. Yet the early poetry is not so unoriginal as it looks. It was *Descriptive Sketches* that first drew Coleridge's attention to Wordsworth, as he tells us in *Biographia Literaria*:

In the form, style, and manner of the whole poem, and in the structure of the particular lines and periods, there is an harshness and acerbity connected and combined with words and images all a-glow, which might recall those products of the vegetable world, where gorgeous blossoms rise out of the hard and thorny rind and shell, within which the rich fruit was elaborating. The language was not only peculiar and strong, but at times knotty and contorted, as by its own impatient strength; while the novelty and struggling crowd of images, acting in conjunction with the difficulties of the style, demanded always a greater closeness of attention, than poetry, (at all events, than descriptive poetry) has a right to claim.[4]

(I.56)

[4]All references to *Biographia Literaria* are to the J. Shawcross edition (Oxford, 1907).

What Coleridge is describing here is a kind of individual voice, powerful and original, which he had detected: and it is true that the verse is full of energy, bursting out of the heroic couplets as a child outgrows its clothes. The subject matter, too, seems too big for the form of these poems: *An Evening Walk*, for instance, is principally about a landscape seen during the course of an afternoon, but it also contains a section in the middle that describes a destitute mother and her starving children. Similarly, *Descriptive Sketches*, which is about Wordsworth's tour of the Alps in 1790, contains a great diversity of material including descriptions of the mountain scenery, reflections on the lot of the Swiss and of mankind in general, and a prophecy of liberty. Both poems look two ways, in fact, to nature and to man, and in this we can see the beginnings of Wordsworth's continuous later concern with the interaction of the two. In these early poems they exist side by side, uncomfortably juxtaposed; in the later poetry there is a creative interaction, so that Wordsworth can portray himself.

On Man, on Nature, and on Human Life,
Musing in solitude . . . .

(preface to *The Excursion*, 1–2)

The introduction of man and human life here is not just a tautology: Wordsworth surveys man, and nature, but also the larger significance that arises from the interaction between the two, between man and the world around him; he is to investigate the nature and purpose of human life, its good and evil, its joy and sorrow. These things are latent in *An Evening Walk* and *Descriptive Sketches*: both are filled with images of the beauty and sublimity of nature, but they are also conscious that mankind, besides having such enjoyments, often has to suffer hardship and misery.

Descriptive Sketches, which was written during Wordsworth's residence in France in 1792, contains a good deal of explicit political suggestion. The 'Salisbury Plain' poems carry this further. They are different versions of the same poem, which ends up in the *Poetical*

Works, somewhat toned down, as 'Guilt and Sorrow,' though part of it was published in the *Lyrical Ballads* under the title of 'The Female Vagrant.' The first Salisbury Plain poem draws its inspiration from Wordsworth's solitary wanderings in 1793 and his angry state of mind at the time: the first version ends with an impassioned plea for revolution and a new order:

Heroes of Truth pursue your march, uptear
Th'Oppressor's dungeon from its deepest base;
High o'er the towers of Pride undaunted rear
Resistless in your might the herculean mace
Of Reason; let foul Error's monster race
Dragged from their dens start at the light with pain
And die; pursue your toils, till not a trace
Be left on earth of Superstition's reign,
Save that eternal pile which frowns on Sarum's plain.
(541–549)

The story of the poem concerns a good-hearted sailor (the first stanzas of the second version show him helping an aged soldier) who has been forced into the navy by a press-gang and dismissed without reward. In his anger he robs and kills a traveller, and now wanders homeless across the plain. In a ruined building he meets a woman, the female vagrant, who relates her story: her father was forced to leave his home by a rapacious landowner, and her husband joined the army to provide for the family; they followed the army to America, where the husband and children all died; and the woman was then shipped back to England. On the following morning the sailor and the vagrant continue their journey, pacifying an angry father who is beating his child, until they meet a dying woman, who turns out to be the sailor's wife; her death affects the sailor so deeply that he gives himself up to justice and is hanged.

In the later published version, entitled 'Guilt and Sorrow,' the sailor is deemed to have suffered enough; in the earlier (second) version, Wordsworth drives home the message of the poem with a remorseless and fixed anger. The female vagrant is one victim of a society that allows the rich to deprive the poor of their livelihood, and in which there is no alternative to poverty but enlistment in the army. The poor and helpless, however benevolent and well disposed, are cast out to fend for themselves, while old soldiers and sailors are thrown on the scrap heap. The sailor is an example of a man who is driven to desperation by the treatment he has received; even more bitter, perhaps, is the way in which at the end, he is surrounded by complacent people who bring him to justice; like the judge in Camus's *L'Etranger*, they make no attempt to understand him. After his death, as he swings in chains on a gibbet, a fair is set up beneath, in a final macabre touch. Meanwhile, the housewife who cares for the dying woman in her last hours stands out as a type of the Good Samaritan, and we are also allowed to see the deep humanity of the sailor and the female vagrant. The sustained anger of the poem is matched only by the poet's admiration for those who can preserve their natural benevolence and kindness in the face of such adversity.

In the years following 1793 this relationship between individual behaviour and the creation of the good society was clearly much in Wordsworth's mind, particularly in view of the later course of the French Revolution. The motives of the Revolution had been so good, and its outcome so disastrous (especially, Wordsworth thought, under Robespierre), that some explanation was desirable. This Wordsworth attempted to supply in *The Borderers*, the other major work of these years. The complicated plot of this tragedy in verse is conducted to a point at which a good man, Marmaduke, is persuaded to leave an old blind man to die in a bleak wasteland; Marmaduke has been deceived by Oswald, who had committed a similar crime many years before, after being manipulated by others. Marmaduke's motives are correct; he is a benevolent man who ends the play in remorse and penitence. Oswald, on the other hand, is driven by his crime to renounce remorse, to see in himself a terrible freedom from normal principles of benevolence and restraint. This is the freedom that he urges upon

Marmaduke, and it was such a freedom that Wordsworth saw a man like Robespierre exercising. 'Let us suppose,' says Wordsworth, describing Oswald in the preface of *The Borderers*, 'a young man of great intellectual powers, yet without any solid principles of genuine benevolence' (*Prose Works*, I.76). His action shows 'the dangerous use which may be made of reason when a man has committed a great crime' (*ibid.*, p. 79). The note to *The Borderers* connects this clearly with the experience in France, for Wordsworth writes that 'sin and crime are apt to start from their very opposite qualities,' and that he had seen this 'while the revolution was rapidly advancing to its extreme of wickedness' (*Poetical Works*, I.342).

When Coleridge heard Wordsworth read *The Borderers* he described it as 'absolutely wonderful' (*Poetical Works*, I.344); he praised the work for its '*profound* touches of the human heart,' seeing in it what later critics have come to recognize as a primary interest of Wordsworth's, the concern with the human heart, traditionally the seat of the affections and the organ of shared feelings between man and man. The concern for the human heart, and for what Wordsworth describes in the preface as 'the primary laws of our nature,' is brilliantly expressed in *Lyrical Ballads*. In *The Borderers* it is tangled up with a complicated plot and an undramatic scenario; in *Lyrical Ballads* it is produced in a marvellous series of spare, taut narrative poems, interwoven with concrete expressions of Wordsworth's own belief and ending with the triumphant 'Tintern Abbey'.

III. LYRICAL BALLADS

Coleridge described Wordsworth's part in *Lyrical Ballads* in his *Biographia Literaria*. While his own energies were to be directed toward the supernatural, Wordsworth

was to propose to himself as his object, to give the charm of novelty to things of every day, and to excite a feeling analogous to the supernatural, by awakening the mind's attention from the lethargy of custom, and directing it to the loveliness and the wonders of the world before us; an inexhaustible treasure, but for which, in consequence of the film of familiarity and selfish solicitude we have eyes, yet see not, ears that hear not, and hearts that neither feel nor understand.   (II.6)

It will be seen that Wordsworth's role was to present the ordinary so that the reader would see it with new eyes; as he said himself about 'The Thorn': 'Cannot I by some invention do as much to make this Thorn permanently an impressive object as the storm has made it to my eyes at this moment?' (*Poetical Works*, II.511). The result is that *Lyrical Ballads* contains many poems that are concerned with simple people in ordinary surroundings, who have problems that are common, sometimes universal: old age, poverty, pregnancy and betrayal, cold, bereavement. Their stories are narrated in a style that is simple and direct, influenced by the street ballads in its dramatic abruptness. This style has sometimes been seen as unsuccessful, as Wordsworth's theory running away with his practice, yet its awkward simplicity is often peculiarly effective. Wordsworth writes a poetry the texture of which allows no escape, which is perhaps why it has been disliked: the lines shock the reader into a recognition of the suffering and the happiness of his fellow human beings, and there is no delicate transfusion of life into art, but, rather, a direct rendering of life into something more tactless and immediate than art. In its spirit it resembles Marianne Moore's poem 'Poetry':

I, too, dislike it: there are things that are important
    beyond all this fiddle.

And yet, paradoxically, Wordsworth's is a highly functioning poetic art, in the sense described by Marianne Moore in her last verse:

... if you demand on the one hand,
the raw material of poetry in
    all its rawness and
    that which is on the other hand
    genuine, then you are interested in poetry.

Wordsworth certainly presents the raw material in all its rawness, in a way that, for many, commands respect; if he leaves himself open to the jeers of the cynic or the sceptic, this is a price he is willing to pay, for the greatest poets have always been vulnerable in this way. So we have Simon Lee's thick ankles, and the little pond in 'The Thorn,' which is three feet long and two feet wide, and poor Betty in 'The Idiot Boy,' 'in a sad distemper.' Not only is there a distinct rawness in these lines, but there is also 'that which is on the other hand genuine,' the respect for the figures who appear in the poems, a respect that comes from love. Wordsworth is well aware of the danger of becoming a voyeur of human suffering: in 'The Thorn,' for instance, he introduces just such a figure, a retired sea-captain who has too little to occupy his time, so that he becomes endlessly curious about his neighbours, and especially about the plight of one of them. We are presented, therefore, with a poem that is at once a narrative and a dramatic monologue; other examples of the sophistication of Wordsworth's art are found in 'The Idiot Boy,' where the diction creates its own rhetorical and rhythmical patterns, and 'Simon Lee,' where the colloquial simplicities of the earlier verses give way to a final quotation that requires the reader to think, sharply and suddenly, to penetrate beneath the conventional complaint of man's ingratitude to something more profound and more pathetic.

It is this respect for his fellow creatures, and this craft, that are the distinguishing marks of *Lyrical Ballads*: they are poems that challenge our very ideas about the nature of poetry and that also confound our expectations in other ways. If we accommodate ourselves to the rhetoric of 'The Idiot Boy,' we are surprised by the ritual game of 'Expostulation and Reply' and 'The Tables Turned,' in which Matthew and William play out a game of statement and counterstatement. If we become accustomed to the simplicity of the ballad style, both in narrative poems and in reflective ones, we are surprised by the majestic reflections of 'Lines Composed a Few Miles Above

Tintern Abbey.' This final poem, the last in the 1798 collection, is written in the eighteenth-century meditative blank-verse style, but with such individuality, originality, and organization as to make it a fitting conclusion to the volume; it should be seen not as the one success in a curious collection but as the open statement of what is explicit or implicit in so many of the other poems, a wonderful openness to feeling and experience. In the preface to *Lyrical Ballads*, published in the second edition (1800), Wordsworth writes of the poet that he is

a man speaking to men: a man, it is true, endowed with more lively sensibility, more enthusiasm and tenderness, who has a greater knowledge of human nature, and a more comprehensive soul, than are supposed to be common among mankind; a man pleased with his own passions and volitions, and who rejoices more than other men in the spirit of life that is in him; delighting to contemplate similar volitions and passions as manifested in the goings-on of the Universe, and habitually impelled to create them where he does not find them.

(*Poetical Works*, II.393)

The importance of this definition is not only in its splendid statement of a shared humanity between the poet and others; it is also concerned with the character of the poet as enthusiast, who is able to express his joy at being alive and finding himself in a world that is full of the same kind of passion and life. To be thus aware of the joy of the world is to be aware also of its variety and complexity, its pain as well as its joy; and Wordsworth is a great tragic poet as well as one who celebrates the happiness of man. He sees the pain of old age, the miseries of poverty, the tragi-comedy of idiocy. The extraordinary feature of *Lyrical Ballads* is that they carry everywhere the evidence of the poet's love for life, for his fellow human beings, for those who are oppressed by society, for his sister, for the natural world around him. This energetic love of life is, in Wordsworth's eyes, evidence of a full humanity; in the preface he describes a poet as 'singing a song in which all human beings join with him' (*Poetical Works*, II.396).

The fundamental conception of the poet as human being, sharing in the joys and sorrows of all mankind with a more than common enthusiasm, has tended to become obscured in the preface by Wordsworth's statements about poetic language. The principal object of *Lyrical Ballads* was, he said,

to choose incidents and situations from common life, and to relate or describe them, throughout, as far as was possible in a selection of language really used by men, and, at the same time, to throw over them a certain colouring of imagination, whereby ordinary things should be presented to the mind in an unusual aspect. . . .

(*ibid.*, II.386)

The phrase 'a selection of language really used by men,' and a similar one from the first paragraph, 'a selection of the real language of men in a state of vivid sensation,' have caused many problems to critics of Wordsworth, from Coleridge onward, who have wanted to know what is meant by 'a selection' or by 'real' language; other difficulties have been posed by those who have solemnly taken Wordsworth to task for what follows:

Humble and rustic life was generally chosen, because, in that condition, the essential passions of the heart find a better soil in which they can attain their maturity, are less under restraint, and speak a plainer and more emphatic language; because in that condition of life our elementary feelings co-exist in a state of greater simplicity, and consequently, may be more accurately contemplated, and more forcibly communicated; because the manners of rural life germinate from those elementary feelings, and, from the necessary character of rural occupations, are more easily comprehended, and are more durable; and, lastly, because in that condition the passions of men are incorporated with the beautiful and permanent forms of nature.

(*ibid.*, II.386-387)

We may disagree with Wordsworth about the need to choose humble and rustic life (although there are clear sociological indications that he may have been right), but his motives are clear and creditable: they are concerned with 'the essential patterns of the heart,' 'elementary

23

feelings,' and 'the passions of men' which are 'incorporated with the beautiful and permanent forms of nature.'
His theory of language (partly set out in the appendix to
the preface) is that primitive poets, although using a
language of extraordinary occasions, spoke a language
'which, though unusual, was still the language of men.' In
the course of time, the unusual became mistaken for the
reality, so that diction became 'daily more and more
corrupt, thrusting out of sight the plain humanities of
nature by a motley masquerade of tricks, quaintnesses,
hieroglyphics, and enigmas' (*Poetical Works*, II.406). It is
clear that Wordsworth was attempting to return to what
he saw as a correct simplicity and directness, and that the
choice of humble and rustic life, together with a
predilection for ordinary language, is connected with this.
The poetic results show how unprejudiced Wordsworth
was about the matter, and how the actual language of his
poetry varied according to the needs of the poem in
question: the language of 'Simon Lee' is very different
from that of 'We Are Seven,' and the impassioned blank
verse of 'Tintern Abbey' is very different from the austere
simplicities of 'Michael.' In every case the aim is to
provide 'little falsehood of description' and ideas
'expressed in language fitted to their respective importance.' So we have the hymnlike utterances of 'To My
Sister':

And from the blessed power that rolls
About, below, above,
We'll frame the measure of our souls:
They shall be tuned to love.

(33–36)

or the nursery rhyme cadences of 'We Are Seven':

I met a little cottage Girl,
She was eight years old, she said;
Her hair was thick with many a curl
That clustered round her head.

(5–8)

The deliberate simplicity of this latter verse is characteristic of some of the shorter poems in *Lyrical Ballads*: critics have often found them naive and oversimple, but Wordsworth was not stupid and clearly had a specific effect in mind, an effect that may not seem as mature or complex as 'Tintern Abbey' but that has an equal importance for an understanding of Wordsworth. He is a poet who is capable of writing with an amazing directness and hard sense, yet he is also capable of writing a poetry that has deeper and more elusive meanings.

As an example of the first kind, we may take 'Simon Lee.' It is a poem that underwent a number of changes after its first publication in 1798, but for convenience I shall take the version that appears in the Oxford Standard Authors edition, by Hutchinson. There the poem begins with a description of Simon Lee as a young man:

In the sweet shire of Cardigan,
Not far from pleasant Ivor-hall
An old Man dwells, a little man,—
'Tis said he once was tall.
Full five-and-thirty years he lived
A running huntsman merry;
And still the centre of his cheek
Is red as a ripe cherry.

                                                    (1–8)

Here the jingle of the rhythm, and the feminine rhyme at the end, encourage a curious jauntiness, an attention such as one gives to a straightforward, cheerful, and undemanding narrative: such a register is even clearer in the 1798 version of the second four lines:

Of years he has upon his back
No doubt, a burthen weighty;
He says he is three score and ten,
But others say he's eighty.

where the random guessing about Simon's age suggests the trivial and simple. In the reworked version of the poem, the first three verses, describing Simon in the past, continue this mood. They describe him as a huntsman in his prime, running, hallooing, and pushing himself to the limit of his endurance. Then comes the change, heralded by a phrase borrowed from Wordsworth's favourite, John Milton:

But, oh the heavy change!—bereft
Of health, strength, friends, and kindred, see!

(25-26)

The same deliberate simplicity is carried on in the following stanzas, which describe the aged and feeble man: it is as though a primitive painter had produced a diptych entitled 'Youth' and 'Age.' Now the reader is given the facts with a hard matter-of-factness:

And he is lean and he is sick;
His body, dwindled and awry,
Rests upon ankles swoln and thick;
His legs are thin and dry.

(33-36)

After this, however, comes a surprise, as the poet himself enters the poem, with a direct address to the reader:

My gentle Reader, I perceive
How patiently you've waited,
And now I fear that you expect
Some tale will be related.

O Reader! had you in your mind
Such stores as silent thought can bring,
O gentle Reader! you would find
A tale in every thing.
What more I have to say is short,
And you must kindly take it:
It is no tale; but, should you think,
Perhaps a tale you'll make it.

(61-72)

Here the style seems to be the same, with the same insistent metre and feminine rhyme; the idea behind these lines, too, seems to be of the same order of simplicity as the earlier descriptive passages, and the continual addressing of the reader has a jocular effect. But beneath the simple words, especially 'tale' and 'think', there lie considerable reverberations. The point of these verses, which contain the central analysis of how to consider Simon Lee and others like him, is that they emphasize the fact that Simon Lee *is*: he is a sad spectacle, an old man past his prime, living on in poverty and unable to perform the simplest task. There is ample matter for the feeling heart to consider here, and there will be no tale, for there should be none: we are contemplating old age, and there will be no escape into a story to take our minds off it. There is, as the poem's subtitle tells us, 'an incident,' but that is all: however, if we *think*, we can make much of that incident, that is, if we have hearts that feel, eyes that perceive, and minds that understand; if, in other words, we *think* about the plight of the elderly, we shall find a deep significance in the trivial incident that follows. It is a significance that is simple because it is universal, containing within itself the awareness of human life as brief, transitory, and often painful. So although it is no story, it contains a deep and inescapable truth:

It is no tale; but, should you think,
Perhaps a tale you'll make it.

The poem is given a final twist, as the traditional complaint against ingratitude is exploited to make something even more pathetic:

—I've heard of hearts unkind, kind deeds
With coldness still returning;
Alas! the gratitude of men
Hath oftener left me mourning.

(93–96)

There are times, it appears, when gratitude is actually worse than ingratitude: from the simplicity of the earlier verses the reader is now faced with a paradox, for the poet grieves more for the pathetic condition of Simon Lee (which makes him weep for the simplest kind of help) than for the usual ingratitude.

If 'Simon Lee' moves from simplicity to a sudden complexity, surprising the reader by its final turn, the movement of 'Tintern Abbey' is much more deliberate, and the poem modulates with consummate skill between different registers of simplicity and complexity. It is a poem that moves between the outer world of nature and the inner world of the mind in a way that beautifully suggests the interaction between the two. There is not space enough here to provide a full examination of the poem, but the way in which its reflective moments alternate with descriptions of the actual landscape is a feature that stands out, although it is most subtly and sensitively accomplished. The poem begins with the river Wye, bounded by its steep and lofty banks, with the pastoral farms and hedgerows, and the quiet sky; at the end the poem comes to rest in the same landscape, with a sense of having gone out and returned that is artistically very satisfying. Between the beginning and end, intertwining with the descriptions of landscape, is the exploration of the poet's mind and heart, and his expressions of confidence and love for his sister and the influence of nature upon her. The poem witnesses to his own experience and his trust that the same blessing will be hers.

The poem is dated 'July 13 1798,' and records a visit to the Wye some five years after the memorable walk of 1793. It records the effect of the landscape on the poet's mind as he remembered it, an effect that is both moral and mystical. The movement of the verse here is characteristic of a certain kind of Wordsworthian blank verse, which begins with a fairly straightforward idea, which it then expands; this leads to a further idea, or a further development, as one moment, or one insight, gives rise to another. The paragraph rises and falls, only to rise higher; the first statements of an idea are taken up and expanded a few lines later ('that blessed mood, . . . that serene and blessed mood'); moments of insight that the reader thinks have been described are suddenly taken up again:

. . . These beauteous forms,
Through a long absence, have not been to me
As is a landscape to a blind man's eye:
But oft, in lonely rooms, and 'mid the din

Of towns and cities, I have owed to them,
In hours of weariness, sensations sweet,
Felt in the blood, and felt along the heart;
And passing even into my purer mind,
With tranquil restoration:— feelings too
Of unremembered pleasure: such, perhaps,
As have no slight or trivial influence
On that best portion of a good man's life,
His little, nameless, unremembered acts
Of kindness and of love. Nor less, I trust,
To them I may have owed another gift,
Of aspect more sublime; that blessed mood,
In which the burthen of the mystery,
In which the heavy and the weary weight
Of all this unintelligible world,
Is lightened:— that serene and blessed mood,
In which the affections gently lead us on,—
Until, the breath of this corporeal frame
And even the motion of our human blood
Almost suspended, we are laid asleep
In body, and become a living soul:
While with an eye made quiet by the power
Of harmony, and the deep power of joy,
We see into the life of things.

(22-49)

The same process is found in the great central passage describing the loss and gain of Wordsworth's imaginative development: if he has lost the dizzy rapture of his first coming to the Wye valley, he has gained a maturity that allows him both to learn and to feel. In this passage the second verb echoes the first, heralding a stronger and more assured statement of an inspiration ('For I have learned ... And I have felt'). The central section is in three parts, rising, declaiming, and descending, with the middle part ('a sense sublime ...') containing a great enveloping conception of the whole of nature as interfused with spirit and movement, with a life that is found in the mind of man and in the external world:

... For I have learned
To look on nature, not as in the hour

Of thoughtless youth; but hearing often-times
The still, sad music of humanity,
Nor harsh nor grating, though of ample power
To chasten and subdue. And I have felt
A presence that disturbs me with the joy
Of elevated thoughts; a sense sublime
Of something far more deeply interfused,
Whose dwelling is the light of setting suns,
And the round ocean and the living air,
And the blue sky, and in the mind of man:
A motion and a spirit, that impels
All thinking things, all objects of all thought,
And rolls through all things . . .

(88–102)

It is tempting to see the impassioned blank verse of
'Tintern Abbey' as the true voice of Wordsworth,
regarding 'Simon Lee' or 'We Are Seven' as unfortunate
applications of a theory of simple language. This is the
theory of Wordsworth as the poet of 'two voices,' which
takes its name from J. K. Stephen's parody of
Wordsworth's own sonnet:

Two voices are there: one is of the deep;
It learns the storm-cloud's thunderous melody,
Now roars, now murmurs with the changing sea,
Now bird-like pipes, now closes soft in sleep;
And one is of an old half-witted sheep
Which bleats articulate monotony,
And indicates that two and one are three,
That grass is green, lakes damp, and mountains steep:
And, Wordsworth, both are thine . . .

This is a sensible and witty view to take, but it ignores so
much of the idiosyncracy that makes Wordsworth
himself and no other: it neglects to observe the way in
which Wordsworth clung tenaciously to the very lines
that seem most ludicrous to modern readers. When his
friend Henry Crabb Robinson told Wordsworth that he
did not dare to read these lines aloud, the poet replied,
'They ought to be liked.' For us to write them off is to
make Wordsworth into our own poet, the poet of
'Tintern Abbey' and the other meditative or narrative

blank verse poems. We would be truer to the spirit of the poet himself if we took *Lyrical Ballads* as a whole and observed it with the spirit that Wordsworth himself had in a letter he wrote in 1802. A young correspondent, John Wilson, had written to him, praising *Lyrical Ballads* but querying the suitability of 'The Idiot Boy,' which he thought not so likely to please. Wordsworth's reply (7 June 1802) was 'please whom? or what?'

I answer, human nature, as it it has been and ever will be. But where are we to find the best measure of this? I answer, from within; by stripping our own hearts naked, and by looking out of ourselves towards men who lead the simplest lives most according to nature men who have never known false refinements, wayward and artificial desires, false criticisms, effeminate habits of thinking and feeling, or who, having known these things, have outgrown them.[5]

And if this is the ideal, the poet is to point to it by leading men toward the good, rather than by reflecting the wishes and feelings of the majority of men:

You have given me praise for having reflected faithfully in my poems the feelings of human nature I would fain hope that I have done so. But a great Poet ought to do more than this he ought to a certain degree to rectify men's feelings, to give them new compositions of feeling, to render their feelings more sane pure and permanent, in short, more consonant to nature, that is, to eternal nature, and the great moving spirit of things. He ought to travel before men occasionally as well as at their sides.

(*ibid.*)

IV. THE PRELUDE

The first attempts at *The Prelude* are found in a small notebook, known as MS.JJ, which Wordsworth used in Germany during the autumn of 1798. By 1799 a two-part

[5]From E. de Selincourt, ed., *Letters of William and Dorothy Wordsworth, The Early Years, 1787–1805*, revised by C. L. Shaver (London, 1967), p. 355.

Prelude of nearly 1,000 lines was complete; this became an almost completed five-book poem, taking the account through the Cambridge years and into the dedication to poetry that is now in Book IV. In 1804 and 1805 Wordsworth added the later books on London, the French Revolution, his despair at its outcome and at the war, and his developing confidence in himself as a poet through the help of Dorothy and Coleridge. The result is the 1805 text, which is the complete poem in thirteen books; this was revised and altered later, with the tenth book divided into two, so that the first publication of the poem in 1850 contained fourteen books. The 1850 text is in some ways more polished, and it contains some fine observations; but the 1805 text (which will be used here) is usually preferred for its freshness and its revelation of Wordsworth's mind at this time.

The Prelude is an extraordinary poem, both in conception and execution, principally because it is epic, history, and autobiography. It is a poem about a single person, a child growing up in the Lake District in the 1770's and 1780's and a young man experiencing the university and the French Revolution; yet it is also much more than this. It contains wonderfully vivid descriptions of the experiences of childhood, but they are contained and given significance by the structure and form of the poem. Basically the poem's experience is one of loss and gain: the loss of the intense childhood experiences and a corresponding gain in maturity and insight. But that experience of loss and gain is set in an epic pattern. In *Paradise Lost*, Milton had written a new kind of epic, as the opening to his book IX shows: Wordsworth, too, is writing a new kind of epic, challenging the traditional concepts of what heroic action consists of. In book III he claims that childhood itself is heroic:

... Of genius, power
Creation and divinity itself
I have been speaking, for my theme has been
What passed within me. Not of outward things
Done visibly for other minds, words, signs,

Symbols or actions, but of my own heart
Have I been speaking, and my youthful mind.
O Heavens! how awful is the might of souls,
And what they do within themselves while yet
The yoke of earth is new to them, the world
Nothing but a wild field where they were sown.
This is, in truth, heroic argument,
And genuine prowess, which I wished to touch
With hand however weak, but in the main
It lies far hidden from the reach of words.

(III.171–185)

The suggestion that the poem's subject is 'Not of outward things' recalls Milton's determination not to write about wars and battles,

... the better fortitude
Of Patience and Heroic Martyrdom
Unsung ...

(*Paradise Lost*, IX.31–33)

Wordsworth carries Milton's innovation a stage further, with an epic treatment of material that is traditionally not associated with the epic; in so doing he claims an epic significance for the growth of a mind, and particularly (as in this case) the growth of a poet's mind. That he had *Paradise Lost* in mind is suggested by an echo at the very beginning of *The Prelude*, where Wordsworth writes

The earth is all before me—with a heart
Joyous, nor scared at its own liberty,
I look about, and should the guide I chuse
Be nothing better than a wandering cloud,
I cannot miss my way ...

(I.15–19)

This takes up the final image of *Paradise Lost*, when Adam and Eve leave Paradise:

The World was all before them, where to choose
Thir place of rest, and Providence thir guide

(XII.646–647)

Where *Paradise Lost* ends, *The Prelude* begins: Milton shows us Adam and Eve at the beginning of human history, faced with the choice of free will and guided by the providence of God; Wordsworth shows us a man in time, able to choose and confident of his ability to use his freedom. In *The Prelude* liberty has replaced the theologians' conception of free will, and the wandering cloud has replaced the workings of Divine Providence: Wordsworth is writing his epic on his own terms of natural goodness and human freedom. What the child does with that freedom is the subject of the early books of *The Prelude*; how the young man survives the pressure of events and retains his imaginative power is the continuation. The whole conception is daring: it is, said Wordsworth, 'a thing unprecedented in literary history that a man should talk so much about himself' (letter to Sir George Beaumont, 1 May 1805). He is, in effect, writing an individual *Paradise Lost*, a poem that sees the life of an obscure country boy in the north west of England as its own kind of significant progress, its own kind of movement from innocence to experience, from paradise to the world outside. Wordsworth makes the reference to *Paradise Lost* clear in a passage of Miltonic pastiche in *The Prelude* (VIII.119–143), a long paragraph of exotic vocabulary and Latinate syntax including a description of Gehol's gardens 'for delight/of the Tartarian Dynasty composed' and the Great Wall of China, 'that mighty Wall, not fabulous, /(China's stupendous mound!).'

Immediately afterwards, Wordsworth swings into his own comparison:

But lovelier far than this the paradise
Where I was reared, in Nature's primitive gifts
Favoured no less, and more to every sense
Delicious, seeing that the sun and sky,
The elements, and seasons in their change,
Do find their dearest fellow-labourer there
The heart of man—a district on all sides
The fragrance breathing of humanity,
Man free, man working for himself, with choice
Of time, and place, and object; by his wants,

His comforts, native occupations, cares,
Conducted on to individual ends
Or social, and still followed by a train,
Unwooed, unthought-of even: simplicity,
And beauty, and inevitable grace.

(VIII.144-158)

The curious sliding movement of the syntax here is not
very common in Wordsworth; but although the elements
occur in apposition, they allow a characteristic accumula-
tion of different effects, so that paradise appeals to the
senses and to the heart of man, and is a place that
encourages the best side of man: man free to work as he
wishes and to live in harmony with himself and his fellow
men. The sense of living as a member of a community is
very important in *The Prelude*: it underlies the happiness
of the early years and the early enthusiasms of the French
Revolution, while the lack of an organic community was
one of the features of London. It is described by
Wordsworth at the beginning of book VII in one of those
homely observations that he does so well:

... Above all, one thought
Baffled my understanding, how men lived
Even next-door neighbours, as we say, yet still
Strangers, and knowing not each other's names.

(VII.117-120)

The Prelude describes this vital sense of a community in a
number of ways. The child himself is part of it and knows
his school friends, the villagers, and the landscape with a
delighted familiarity. There are many instances of this,
but perhaps the most vivid is the opening of Book IV,
where Wordsworth describes the feelings of a university
student coming home for the long vacation. He bounds
down the hill, shouting for the old ferryman, who greets
him; he walks on a few miles to Hawkshead, where he sees
the familiar church; he is welcomed, with tears of joy, by
Ann Tyson and walks around the village with her,
greeting everybody. He sees the old rooms, the old
garden, the boxed-in stream; he takes his place at the well-

loved table and sleeps in his accustomed bed. The whole
first section of book IV is a most beautiful re-creation of
the emotions of coming home to a well-known landscape
and a well-loved community; it looks back, of course, to
the scenes of books I and II, especially to the passages that
describe the children playing together, skating, or playing
cards with the battered and dirty pack (the cards
themselves cherished like old soldiers), or rowing or
riding. It looks forward, too, to the hopes for the French
Revolution as the beginning of the new Jerusalem:

> For, born in a poor district, and which yet
> Retaineth more of ancient homeliness,
> Manners erect, and frank simplicity,
> Than any other nook of English land,
> It was my fortune scarcely to have seen
> Through the whole tenor of my schoolday time
> The face of one, who, whether boy or man,
> Was vested with attention or respect
> Through claims of wealth or blood; . . .
>
> . . . It could not be
> But that one tutored thus, who had been formed
> To thought and moral feeling in the way
> This story hath described, should look with awe
> Upon the faculties of man, receive
> Gladly the highest promises, and hail
> As best the government of equal rights
> And individual worth . . .
>
> (IX.217–226; 242–249)

The Prelude, then, is an epic that deals with the loss of
paradise; it is Wordsworth's childhood seen as myth, in
that he has constructed around his own experience a
reading of events that corresponds to the paradise myth.
We know that he was not happy at Penrith, and we can
only guess at the effect of his mother's death when he was
eight and his father's when he was thirteen. Both of these
are referred to in *The Prelude*, but not until Books V and
XI respectively, and there is nothing in the early books to
suggest unhappiness and bereavement. There is fear, but

that is accepted – indeed, welcomed – as part of the educative ministry of nature:

Fair seed-time had my soul, and I grew up
Fostered alike by beauty and by fear

(I.305–306)

but the individual development through beauty and fear is supported by the sense that the individual is part of the community. He can be himself, but he can also be one of a number, as the skating episode shows. The pronouns shift from singular to plural in a way that conveys the mixture of individual impression and communal feeling:

... All shod with steel
We hissed along the polished ice in games
Confederate, imitative of the chace
And woodland pleasures, the resounding horn,
The pack loud bellowing, and the hunted hare.
So through the darkness and the cold we flew,
And not a voice was idle. With the din,
Meanwhile, the precipices rang aloud;
The leafless trees and every icy crag
Tinkled like iron; while the distant hills
Into the tumult sent an alien sound
Of melancholy, not unnoticed; while the stars,
Eastward, were sparkling clear, and in the west
The orange sky of evening died away.

Not seldom from the uproar I retired
Into a silent bay, or sportively
Glanced sideway, leaving the tumultuous throng,
To cut across the image of a star
That gleamed upon the ice. And oftentimes
When we had given our bodies to the wind,
And all the shadowy banks on either side
Came sweeping through the darkness, spinning still
The rapid line of motion, then at once
Have I, reclining back upon my heels,
Stopped short—yet still the solitary cliffs
Wheeled by me, even as if the earth had rolled
With visible motion her diurnal round.
Behind me did they stretch in solemn train,
Feebler and feebler, and I stood and watched
Till all was tranquil as a dreamless sleep.   (I.460–489)

In this brilliant passage, with its wonderful recreation of the movement and sound of skating, and of a Lake District winter twilight, the child is sharing in the experience and in the delight of a game with the others. Yet he is also able to retire 'into a silent bay,' and to perceive the way the earth seems to move, at a sudden stop. Like the poet of the preface to *Lyrical Ballads*, he is a child speaking to (or for) children, yet also a child endowed with more lively sensibility, rejoicing more than others in the spirit of life that is in him. The joyful energy of this passage is one of its most obvious characteristics, tempered as it is with a solemn awareness of the beauty and majesty of the earth. *The Prelude* as a whole is a striking combination of these qualities of individual energy and delight, with an equally important sense that the mind of the poet is, in many ways, a representative mind. It is aware, as we have seen, of the importance of the community; and the poem is also concerned with a major historical event, the French Revolution, an event of which the hopes and disappointments dominated the Romantic movement. In the books on France, Wordsworth is recording the fact that he was present at the Revolution's various stages: when he first landed in France, on 13 July 1790, he and Robert Jones saw 'benevolence and blessedness/ Spread like a fragrance everywhere, like Spring' (VI.368-369). He had the enthusiasm and optimism of youth:

Bliss was it in that dawn to be alive,
But to be young was very heaven! ...

(X.692-693)

and this optimism was based upon observations, upon conversations with Beaupuy, upon a direct experience of a nation struggling to find its new liberty. In Book X, Wordsworth relates, with a painful authenticity, how he was torn in sympathy when prayers for an English victory were offered in church, and how his attitudes to the Revolution changed as the French became 'oppressors in their turn' (X.791). He describes how he studied the problem relentlessly,

```
          . . . endlessly perplexed
With impulse, motive, right and wrong, the ground
Of moral obligation—what the rule,
And what the sanction—till, demanding proof,
And seeking it in every thing, I lost
All feeling of conviction, and, in fine,
Sick, wearied out with contrarieties,
Yielded up moral questions in despair . . .
                                            (X.893-900)
```

Book X of *The Prelude* is a most impressive record of a sensitive mind in confrontation with the great political events of the day: not only the French Revolution and the war, but the campaign for the abolition of the slave trade (X.202-226). He saw revolution become madness, and the rise and fall of Robespierre, with all the intense involvement of a contemporary; he remembered exactly where he was when he heard of the death of Robespierre, crossing Ulverston sands after visiting the grave of his beloved schoolmaster, William Taylor, at Cartmel. The scene (X.466-566), with the smooth sands of the Leven estuary in the foreground and the Lake District mountains in the background, is one of the most vividly pictorialized in *The Prelude*; the moment when the passing traveller told him that Robespierre was dead is sharpened by the poet's awareness of his surroundings and his feelings. It is no accident, of course, that the death of Robespierre is told to Wordsworth just after he had been thinking of the death of Taylor: the one famous and tyrannical, the other obscure and benevolent. In ways such as this, *The Prelude* is a record of what it was like to live through those years, to be a child at Hawkshead, a young man at Cambridge, a spectator in London, and an enthusiast in France.

Above all, however, these roles or stages were seen by Wordsworth in *The Prelude* as part of the growth of a poet's mind (the poem's alternative title). And if the poem is about the paradise myth, with the child growing up in the good community, and about history, with the child and young man responding to historical and social conditions around him, it is also about the development of a very special and very gifted man. Once again, it is possible to see Wordsworth referring back to Milton, who saw the role of the poet as a prophet or inspired teacher. In *Il Penseroso* the poet longs for the learning and wisdom of old age:

Till old experience do attain
To something like Prophetic strain.

(173–174)

and in *Paradise Lost* he remembers other figures who have suffered the same fate as himself, the loss of sight—

So were I equal'd with them in renown,
Blind *Thamyris* and blind *Maeonides*,
And *Tiresias* and *Phineus* Prophets old.

(III.34–36)

Wordsworth, too, uses the word 'Prophet'; and in some ways the whole of *The Prelude* can be seen as moving toward the final paragraph, in which he sees himself and Coleridge as engaged in the teaching of mankind:

Prophets of Nature, we to them will speak
A lasting inspiration, sanctified
By reason and by truth; what we have loved
Others will love, and we may teach them how:
Instruct them how the mind of man becomes
A thousand times more beautiful than the earth
On which he dwells, above this frame of things
(Which, 'mid all revolutions in the hopes
And fears of men, doth still remain unchanged)
In beauty exalted, as it is itself
Of substance and of fabric more divine.

(XIII.442–452)

It is toward this end, with the poet as a responsible member of society and an inspired teacher, that so much of *The Prelude* has been moving. The range of experience that contributes to this is considerable, including the childhood episodes, education, books, and the sublime experiences that remain in the memory long after they have passed. Wordsworth calls them 'spots of time' in a crucial passage:

> There are in our existence spots of time,
> Which with distinct preeminence retain
> A renovating virtue, whence, depressed
> By false opinion and contentious thought,
> Or aught of heavier or more deadly weight
> In trivial occupations and the round
> Of ordinary intercourse, our minds
> Are nourished and invisibly repaired—
> A virtue, by which pleasure is enhanced,
> That penetrates, enables us to mount
> When high, more high, and lifts us up when fallen.
>
> (XI.257-267)

Such moments, he goes on to say, are 'scattered everywhere' (XI.274), though they may be most conspicuous in childhood; he gives an example of two episodes that are vividly remembered, being lost and finding himself beneath a murderer's gibbet, and waiting for the horses to take him home just before his father's death. In both cases there is a mysterious intensity about the episode, a moment of perception that remains with extraordinary sharpness. In the first, the child, regaining the path, sees

> A naked pool that lay beneath the hills,
> The beacon on the summit, and more near,
> A girl who bore a pitcher on her head
> And seemed with difficult steps to force her way
> Against the blowing wind. . . .
>
> (XI.303-307)

The poet recalls how he later revisited the spot and remembered the earlier occasion:

> . . . So feeling comes in aid
> Of feeling, and diversity of strength
> Attends us, if but once we have been strong.
>
> (XI.325-327)

We recognize this as one of Wordsworth's complex states, in which 'feeling comes in aid/ Of feeling.' He is not clear exactly why the force of the episode is so great, but he knows that it is: the greatness of man is mysterious and deep, and it is by the exploration of such episodes that we come to understand and acknowledge it. As a child, the poet was lost; as an adult, looking back, he now says:

I am lost, but see
In simple childhood something of the base
On which thy greatness stands—but this I feel,
That from thyself it is that thou must give,
Else never canst receive ...

(XI.329–333)

The sentiment is reminiscent of Coleridge's 'we receive but what we give' (from the 'Letter to Sara Hutchinson'), and it indicates something of the interacting relationship between the mind and the external world that was so important to both poets. In their most confident moments, both poets felt a great union between man and nature, a profound interaction, or what Wordsworth describes as a 'consummation' between the human mind and the natural world. Sometimes this comes at unexpected moments, as it does in the second 'spot of time' in Book XI. This describes the poet and his brothers waiting for the horses to take them home at Christmas time: through the misty day he waited beside a stone wall, with a single sheep and a hawthorn tree for company (it is remarkable how often single trees or lonely people and animals occur in Wordsworth). He had been so impatient to get home, the poet records, and then ten days later his father died; he saw himself tritely as punished for his impatience, though clearly this is not the point of the passage. The long wait in the mist and rain, the strange company of sheep and tree (in his impatience he had left his brothers further down the pass), these constituents of the moment remained with him as a testimony to his imaginative grasp of a situation:

And afterwards the wind and sleety rain,
And all the business of the elements,

The single sheep, and the one blasted tree,
And the bleak music of that old stone wall,
The noise of wood and water, and the mist
Which on the line of each of these two roads
Advanced in such indisputable shapes—
All these were spectacles and sounds to which
I often would repair, and thence would drink
As at a fountain. . . .

(XI.375-384)

In this description we notice not only the emphasis on the particular objects (the wind, the rain, the single sheep, the blasted tree) but an emphasis on what Wordsworth elsewhere calls the 'goings-on' of the physical world. He animates the dreariness with unobtrusive life: 'all the business of the elements,' 'the bleak music of that old stone wall,' 'The noise of wood and water,' the mist that 'Advanced in such indisputable shapes,' all these suggest a mind that goes out to the universe and responds to what it is doing – a mind that apprehends the 'business,' hears the 'music,' and sees the shapes of the mist. Wordsworth is here celebrating not the power of nature, but the power of the imagination and the memory.

The same can be said of two other great passages in *The Prelude* that are concerned with the growth of the inspired prophet-poet. The first is the crossing of the Alps section in Book VI (494 and following). Once again, as in the 'spots of time' moments of Book XI, there is a loss of direction, a momentary sense of failure, an unfulfilled expectation; as in those 'spots of time,' the failure and loss, the mistaken hope, are suddenly transformed into an awareness of the power of the imagination. In book VI, it is addressed directly, in a startling apostrophe that erupts into the verse:

Imagination!—lifting up itself
Before the eye and progress of my song
Like an unfathered vapour, here that power,
In all the might of its endowments, came
Athwart me. I was lost as in a cloud,
Halted without a struggle to break through,

And now, recovering, to my soul I say
'I recognize thy glory'. In such strength
Of usurpation, in such visitings
Of awful promise, when the light of sense
Goes out in flashes that have shewn to us
The invisible world, doth greatness make abode,
There harbours whether we be young or old.
Our destiny, our nature, and our home,
Is with infinitude—and only there;
With hope it is, hope that can never die,
Effort, and expectation, and desire,
And something evermore about to be.

(VI.525–542)

Here the imagination itself is like a vapour or mist; the poet seems overcome by it, lost in it as he was on the Alpine path. But he suddenly sees the power of the imagination, not in the fact but in the promise, not in the material world but in the glimpse of something higher and beyond. As he sees this he becomes aware of the sheer power of an imagination that can so transcend its material circumstances as to become conscious of its activity. Similarly, in the 'climbing of Snowdon' passage from the final book of *The Prelude*, the poet describes a night climb from Bethgelert through the mist, until suddenly he and his companions came out of the mist into the moonlight. They found themselves surrounded by a sea of mist, out of which the Welsh hills lifted their peaks and over which the moon looked down 'in single glory.' So strong is the impression of the mist as a sea that Wordsworth has to describe it as moving eventually

Into the sea, the real sea. . . .

(XIII.49)

The fact that Wordsworth has to describe it as 'the real sea' is a testimony of how powerful his imagination has become. Before, the real world existed, and the imagination erupted from it; now the imagination seems to be supreme, and the real world has to be admitted. Between the mountain and the shore is a chasm, a fracture in the mist:

44

A deep and gloomy breathing-place through which
Mounted the roar of waters, torrents, streams
Innumerable, roaring with one voice.

(XIII.57–59)

The stupendous natural vision is one that Wordsworth
sees as an emblem of the power of the mind; only with
such a powerful landscape can he begin to say what the
mind is capable of doing:

... it appeared to me
The perfect image of a mighty mind,
Of one that feeds upon infinity,
That is exalted by an under-presence,
The sense of God, or whatsoe'er is dim
Or vast in its own being—above all,
One function of such mind had Nature there
Exhibited by putting forth, and that
With circumstance most awful and sublime:
That domination which she oftentimes
Exerts upon the outward face of things,
So moulds them, and endues, abstracts, combines,
Or by abrupt and unhabitual influence
Doth make one object so impress itself
Upon all others, and pervades them so,
That even the grossest minds must see and hear,
And cannot chuse but feel. ...

(XIII.68–84)

The imaginative minds are ever on the watch, building up
greatness from the least suggestion, or from failure, or
from ordinary expectations that have come to grief. This,
the poet concludes, 'this alone is genuine liberty'
(XIII.122); the ability of the mind to transcend its
surroundings, to become aware, even when it is least
expected, of the strength of the imagination. For often it
surprises, and surprise is a favourite idea of Wordsworth's.
Moments come upon the imagination with strange
suddenness: as the child rows a stolen boat out from the
shore at Patterdale, he is astonished and terrified to see
the mountain coming after him; as the child who is
hooting to the owls (V.389 and following) fails to get a
response, he is suddenly aware of something else:

Then sometimes in that silence, while he hung
Listening, a gentle shock of mild surprise
Has carried far into his heart the voice
Of mountain torrents; or the visible scene
Would enter unawares into his mind
With all its solemn imagery, its rocks,
Its woods, and that uncertain heaven, received
Into the bosom of the steady lake.

(V.406–413)

Here the mind receives, but it receives because it is a mind that can give. The boy of Winander hooting to the owls is contrasted throughout Book V with the fact-getting, well-behaved, unnatural child; the boy who died young was one of those with whom Wordsworth played:

A race of real children, not too wise,
Too learned, or too good, but wanton, fresh,
And bandied up and down by love and hate;
Fierce, moody, patient, venturous, modest, shy,
Mad at their sports like withered leaves in winds;
Though doing wrong and suffering, and full oft
Bending beneath our life's mysterious weight
Of pain and fear, yet still in happiness
Not yielding to the happiest upon earth.

(V.436–444)

And so, as so often with Wordsworth, the greatest sublimity is linked with the celebration of the ordinary; and to pursue the development of the prophet-poet, and the great creative imagination, is to be reminded that they are rooted in an ordinary childhood. It is all wonderfully simple, yet wonderfully mysterious and profound:

Oh mystery of man, from what a depth
Proceed thy honours! I am lost, but see
In simple childhood something of the base
On which thy greatness stands— . . .

(XI.328–331)

and the greatness of *The Prelude* is that it does succeed in testifying to the power of the imagination while being firmly rooted in human experience.

V. SHORTER POEMS AFTER 1798

The sheer ordinariness that is an essential part of Wordsworth is continued in the poems written after *Lyrical Ballads*; yet it is an ordinariness transformed, as in *The Prelude*, by an imaginative balance that seems to achieve just the right adjustment between the subject matter and its transformation.

In the 'Lucy' poems, for instance, most of which were written in Germany during the winter of 1798-1799, Wordsworth writes of the death of a young girl who is an embodiment of all the natural forces of simplicity and grace. In one poem she is a 'flower' and 'sportive as the fawn'; she lives in the poet's memory as an ideal figure who has died while she is still in a fresh and youthful state of communion with nature. In the greatest of these poems, 'A Slumber Did My Spirit Seal,' she is first an ideal, almost spiritual creature and then a dead girl; yet even then she is reunited with nature in a way that seems appropriate and that turns her death into a fitting reunion with the world of which she was a part. She is both girl and nature form, shaped and moulded by a force outside her; the poet sees her for a time, and loves her, only to lose her. Thus the 'Lucy' poems are both elegies for a loved one and something more, a perception of an ideal and an indication of the transience of natural innocence. In his description of *Lyrical Ballads* in *Biographia Literaria*, Coleridge wrote of 'the two cardinal points of poetry':

... the power of exciting the sympathy of the reader by a faithful adherence to the truth of nature, and the power of giving the interest of novelty by the modifying colours of imagination.

(II.5)

This is a remarkable insight into the working of Wordsworth's shorter poems: they are true to nature, that is, to a visible and recognizable external world, and yet that world is given a significance that it normally lacks. The significance is given to it by the perceiving mind, which allows the thing or person to be seen more vividly and yet as something more than its material self. So the sheepfold in 'Michael' remains a sheepfold but becomes a symbol of all the unfulfilled hopes of the shepherd's life, and of more than that: it is a symbol and not an allegorical representation of something. So it has a life of its own: it exists in the eye of the passer-by as he walks up the path beside Green-head Ghyll, and it has a history that sums up the whole life and fate of Michael and his family. They are simple, frugal people, who prefer to remain on the land rather than sell it to pay off the indemnity; Michael's work is with the elements, among the fields and hills, and he is summoned to work by the winds. His feelings, too, are elementary passions of the kind that Wordsworth saw as existing among rustic folk: his tenderness for his son and his love of the land on which he has worked all his life. The laying of the cornerstone of the sheepfold, done by Luke at his request, is an act of faith and hope: the sheepfold becomes a covenant between the father and the son but also, in its way, an act of defiance against the destructiveness of the monetary and city world. Michael and Luke are forced to separate, and Luke comes to grief: Michael continues to go to the sheepfold, but he is unable to finish it, although he continues to work at it. The celebrated line

And never lifted up a single stone

(466)

has tended to make the reader forget that in fact Michael did continue to work at the sheepfold for seven years after Luke's downfall. Michael is a man of determination and perseverance; his life has been one of industrious labour, and the downfall of Luke does not alter this. But he has no heart to continue at times when the grief is too great; the sheepfold is an emblem of his purpose in life, the construction of something that will survive for Luke, as he hoped that the patrimonial fields would pass to him. Instead, in the city, Luke

... gave himself
To evil courses: ignominy and shame

48

Fell on him, so that he was driven at last
To seek a hiding-place beyond the seas.

(444–447)

In this poem, the sheepfold and the cottage are the
foreground, and city is far away; Luke's downfall is
portrayed with a brisk absence of detail, whereas
Michael's speeches are recorded verbatim. It is a masterly
use of perspective to emphasize the quality of life and the
destruction that comes into it from outside; as we know
from *The Prelude*, Wordsworth had a particular admiration for shepherds, and 'Michael' is a narrative poem that
records the way in which the shepherd and his wife seem
hardly to understand other ways. They are touchingly
naive about Luke's departure, and presumably about life
and conditions in the city; yet their naiveté is associated
throughout with love. Michael loves the land and has an
abiding love for Luke. He promises the boy that

> '. . . whatever fate
> Befall thee, I shall love thee to the last,
> And bear thy memory with me to the grave.'

(415–417)

So too, after the brief account of Luke's fall, comes the
resounding line

> There is a comfort in the strength of love;

(448)

which indicates the contrary movements of love and
despair that exist within Michael: he is a man who has
experienced a lifetime of love, in his work and its
surroundings, in the domestic happiness of his frugal
home, in his land, and in the tenderness of his relationship
with his son. When the last of these is broken the others
remain; as so often in Wordsworth, the figures who are
bereft of human relationships retain a strange and lonely
dignity that comes from an affinity with nature. Michael
is deeply moving because he represents every aging father
with an only child in whom his hopes are centred; he is
also awesome in his ability to go on loving. He is a man for

whom the reader feels not tragic pity and fear but a mixture of pity and admiration.

The same is true of other solitaries in Wordsworth, most notably the leech-gatherer in 'Resolution and Independence.' If 'Michael' is written in an austere and stately blank verse (for although the metre is the same, the language is quite different from the impassioned diction of 'Tintern Abbey'), 'Resolution and Independence' is written in stanza form, with a peculiar and very effective diction. It is metrically very formal, with an alexandrine at the end of each stanza, and the diction is often archaic, with a Biblical cadence and rhythm:

Motionless as a cloud the old Man stood,
That heareth not the loud winds when they call;
And moveth all together, if it move at all.

(75–77)

The use of subjunctives ('if it move') and the older forms of the verb (heareth, moveth) are linked with rhythms that echo Biblical ones ('consider the lilies of the field, how they grow': 'That heareth not the loud winds when they call'). The result is a poem that describes an encounter with a poor old man in formal and stately terms, so that the old man himself is given dignity. In Dorothy Wordsworth's journal, he appears as 'an old man almost double':

He had on a coat, thrown over his shoulders, above his waistcoat and coat. Under this he carried a bundle, and had an apron on and a night-cap . . . . His trade was to gather leeches, but now leeches are scarce, and he had not strength for it. He lived by begging. . . .

(3 October 1800)

When Wordsworth wrote 'Resolution and Independence' some eighteen months later (in the productive spring of 1802), any of these details that might make the old man seem ludicrous were carefully removed. He enters the poem now at a moment when the poet is gloomily contemplating his own future: it is a brilliant fresh morning after rain, yet the poet feels uncertain about the fate of fellow poets and his own failure to provide; like the grasshopper in the fable, his whole life has been lived 'in pleasant thought,/ As if life's business were a summer mood' (36–37). Instead of being made to regret this by the hard-working ant, however, he meets the leech-gatherer, whose appearance is preceded by words such as 'grace':

Now, whether it were by peculiar grace,
A leading from above, a something given,
Yet it befell that, in this lonely place,
When I with these untoward thoughts had striven,
Beside a pool bare to the eye of heaven
I saw a Man before me unawares:
The oldest man he seemed that ever wore grey hairs.

(50–56)

The great simplicities of Wordsworth's poetry appear to wonderful effect in a line like 'I saw a Man . . . . ,' especially as Wordsworth goes on to qualify this:

As a huge stone is sometimes seen to lie
Couched on the bald top of an eminence;
Wonder to all who do the same espy,
By what means it could thither come, and whence;
So that it seems a thing endued with sense:
Like a sea-beast crawled forth, that on a shelf
Of rock or sand reposeth, there to sun itself. . . .

(57–63)

Here the old man is likened to a stone and to a strange sea beast; or, to complicate the process, he could be said to be likened to a stone that itself is like a sea beast. Either way, here is a strange combination of inanimate and animate, as though the old man is half immobile and insensate, and half strangely alive. It is interesting, too, to see how the rhythm of the line unobtrusively emphasizes the strangeness of the old man. He is like a stone 'Couched on the bald top of an eminence,' where the words 'bald top' give two strong syllables in the middle of the line. Without the word 'bald,' the line would be regularly dactylic, with three feet:

Couched on the top of an eminence

With 'bald,' it becomes strangely out of joint, especially when followed by the trochaic 'Wonder' in the following line. But Wordsworth unerringly brings the reader back to the reality in the following line:

Such seemed this Man, . . .

which echoes 'I saw a Man' and allows all the strangeness of the earlier verse to be clamped between the two occurrences of 'Man'. The man's humanity is asserted, even, it might be said, his basic humanity: he is Man, old and unaccommodated, and the poet's meeting with him has something of the meeting of the sophisticated with the elementary or primitive. The old man's physical condition is miserable: he is bent double with age, and like the stone-*cum*-sea beast, he seems 'not all alive nor dead.' Yet he returns a courteous answer to the poet's greeting, and replies to his inquiry 'what are you doing?' The poet describes him thus:

Ere he replied, a flash of mild surprise
Broke from the sable orbs of his yet-vivid eyes.

His words came feebly, from a feeble chest,
But each in solemn order followed each,
With something of a lofty utterance drest—

(90–94)

The understated skill of Wordsworth's verse is brilliantly demonstrated here, in the contrast between the rhetorical and poetic language of the first two and the last two lines here, and the strong simplicity of the middle line. In the first two lines the diction ('sable orbs,' 'yet-vivid eyes') might have come from Milton; so might the image of words following each other dressed in their lofty utterance. In the centre is the line full of effort, with the repetition of 'feebly . . . feeble,' the alliteration of which suggests a difficulty in breathing or speaking freely. The contrast embodies the whole sense of strangeness that is found within the poem, the coexistence of an internal state that does not match the external conditions. The poet is miserable on a beautiful morning; the decrepit man is firm in his courage and his optimism. As he describes his condition to the poet (and it is noticeable that in this version he is no longer begging) the poet becomes curiously abstracted; it is as though the individual situation becomes lost in its wider implications:

The old Man still stood talking by my side;
But now his voice to me was like a stream
Scarce heard; nor word from word could I divide;
And the whole body of the Man did seem
Like one whom I had met with in a dream;
Or like a man from some far region sent,
To give me human strength, by apt admonishment.

(106–112)

The idea of the old man as having been sent 'from some far region' links up with the earlier description of him as 'a something given'; he seems to be both natural and in some way supernatural. He comes to bring the poet human strength, yet in the last verse the poet turns to God:

'God,' said I, 'be my help and stay secure;
I'll think of the Leech-gatherer on the lonely moor!'

(139–140)

The leech-gatherer seems to stand for something, or rather to be something, above and beyond the customary experience and certainly above the worldly cares of the poet. It would be a great mistake to see him as an allegory of some kind of religious presence, but he is clearly an indication of something outside the poet, a strength and a resolution that contrasts forcibly with the poet's own failure to keep a serene mind. The leech-gatherer, in fact, embodies qualities that Wordsworth signally admired: an independence and a serenity that freed him from financial and other worldly responsibilities; this liberty is, for Wordsworth, a true freedom from anxiety, and it is connected with other freedoms that he celebrates in his poetry.

Politically, a love of freedom made him a supporter of the French Revolution, and later a fervent patriot; in social terms he admired societies like the one he had known in his youth, where men seemed to be independent and not bound together in a master-slave relationship; and in personal terms, he sought a freedom from anxiety, a freedom that does not seek to avoid misfortune but that comes from having the resources to bear it. Meanwhile, the relationship between this ideal freedom and the actual world of man continues to exercise Wordsworth; the ideal world is found in many forms, especially associated with nature and childhood, and the poet's delight in it is found in many of the poems written in these years, especially in the spring of 1802. Many of these poems, 'The Tinker,' 'To a Butterfly,' 'Among All Lovely Things My Love Had Been,' 'To the Small Celandine,' celebrate happiness and freedom, while others are aware of the forces that destroy these things. 'The Sailor's Mother' is one, and the 'Ode. Intimations of Immortality from Recollections of Early Childhood' is another. The great Ode, as it is sometimes called, balances a marvellous recapturing of the child's innocence and closeness to nature with an awareness of the later perception of an adult; the poet laments the inevitable process of growing into adulthood, embraced so enthusiastically by the child who acts grown-up parts, and yet the Ode is informed by a mature and responsible understanding that this process is necessary. A Neo-platonic sense of a reality elsewhere is joined to the memory of the child's experience, and through it our life on earth is seen to be an absence from a home in God. Yet the life on earth has its own precious moments, and not only in childhood:

The thought of our past years in me doth breed
  Perpetual benediction. . . .

(137–138)

The benediction comes not just from the memory of delight and liberty, but from something more elusive and profound:

. . . those obstinate questionings
Of sense and outward things,

Fallings from us, vanishings;
  Blank misgivings of a Creature
Moving about in worlds not realised,
High instincts before which our mortal Nature
Did tremble like a guilty Thing surprised. . . .

(145–151)

With this praise for the mysterious and marvellous, there
is another source of comfort, in the strength that the
adult gains through contemplating life in all its confusion
and limitations:

In the primal sympathy
Which having been must ever be;
In the soothing thoughts that spring
Out of human suffering;
In the faith that looks through death,
In years that bring the philosophic mind.

(185–190)

The great Ode is a key poem in the understanding of the
complexity of Wordsworth's beliefs. It contains, without
fracturing into different pieces, the joy in childhood and
liberty, the unity of this with the rejoicing natural world,
and the sense, too, of the mature understanding of the
role of man in the created world. The child is a prophet;
the man can only remember, and understand, but his view
of life involves an accommodation with things as they are
that is a gain to compensate for the loss of the childhood
vision.

Wordsworth's belief in the faith that looks through
death was tested to the uttermost in February 1805, when
his favourite brother, John, was drowned at sea. In his
grief the poet turned to a favourite subject, the daisy, the
'unassuming Common-place/ Of Nature,' which he saw
as sleeping and waking upon the sailor's grave; even here
there is a comfort from the simple things of nature. But in
a greater poem, 'Elegiac Stanzas, Suggested by a Picture
of Peele Castle, in a Storm, Painted by Sir George
Beaumont,' Wordsworth chronicled a change. He had
stayed near Peele Castle in fine weather, in 1794; now he
saw Beaumont's picture, which showed it in a very

different condition: a ruined tower beaten by the waves
(the painting also contained a ship going down offshore,
which would have reminded Wordsworth of his brother's
death). The stormy sea he now sees as the true reflector of
the condition of life, and the idea of a world governed by
fine weather has disappeared:

A power is gone, which nothing can restore;
A deep distress hath humanised my Soul.

(35–36)

As so often with Wordsworth, loss is turned into gain,
and he sees himself as becoming more human and less
likely to idealize in his bereavement. Certainly his poetry,
from this time on, becomes less elusive and imaginative:
even 'Peele Castle' has an allegorical construction that is
uncomfortably schematic – fine weather contrasted with
bad weather, the castle standing against the storms of life,
the sense of a 'before' and 'after' scene. It is saved by its
austere diction and its stern sense of mourning tempered
by hope:

Farewell, farewell the heart that lives alone,
Housed in a dream, at distance from the Kind!
Such happiness, wherever it be known,
Is to be pitied; for 'tis surely blind.

But welcome fortitude, and patient cheer,
And frequent sights of what is to be borne!
Such sights, or worse, as are before me here.—
Not without hope we suffer and we mourn.

(53–60)

VI. SONNETS, THE EXCURSION, AND LATER POEMS

The 'Elegiac Stanzas,' 'Resolution and Independence,'
the 'Immortality Ode,' and many of Wordsworth's best-
known shorter poems (such as 'The Solitary Reaper' and
'I Wandered Lonely as a Cloud') were published in
Poems, in Two Volumes in 1807. This volume also

contains some of Wordsworth's finest sonnets, a form in which he delighted. Once again his great master was Milton, and both poets use the same Italianate form, revelling in its compression and the artistic demands of its rhyme scheme. 'Nuns fret not at their convent's narrow room,' wrote Wordsworth, and he seems to have relished the discipline required to produce a good sonnet. Among the sonnets are some of the best patriotic poetry ever written, which links a love of England with qualities of spiritual nobility, as in 'Milton! thou shouldst be living at this hour.' The arresting first line is a feature of Wordsworth's sonnets: 'Earth has not anything to show more fair' is perhaps the best-known example, but there are others, such as 'Once did She hold the gorgeous east in fee' (another sonnet on a political subject, the extinction of the Venetian republic by Napoleon) and 'It is a beauteous evening, calm and free.' In this last example, the sonnet continues with a literally breathtaking image

> The holy time is quiet as a Nun
> Breathless with adoration; . . .
>
> (2-3)

and then, as so often, Wordsworth anchors the image in straightforward natural description—

> . . . the broad sun
> Is sinking down in its tranquillity;
>
> (3-4)

—only to invite the imagination to work again by the use of figurative language:

> The gentleness of heaven broods o'er the Sea:
> Listen! the mighty Being is awake,
> And doth with his eternal motion make
> A sound like thunder—everlastingly.
>
> (5-8)

It is not clear to whom the word 'Listen!' is addressed. Its introduction here gives it a general sense, as though anyone on a calm evening might, by listening, hear the workings of a mighty Being. But it then acquires a particular meaning, as Wordsworth turns to address his French daughter:

Dear Child! dear Girl! that walkest with me here,
If thou appear untouched by solemn thought,
Thy nature is not therefore less divine:
Thou liest in Abraham's bosom all the year;
And worshipp'st at the Temple's inner shrine,
God being with thee when we know it not.

(9–14)

There is a very delicate change of mood here, from the impersonal to the personal, with an equalizing movement from the ordinary to the sacred. A further balancing is found between the tender and the reflective as the poet notes the distance between the child's unconscious communion with heaven and her conscious ordinariness. The difference between the child's apparent state, walking the sands with a mind 'untouched by solemn thought,' and her actual state is underlined by the biblical formality of the last lines, which apply to the child in a mysterious and remote, yet authoritative way. Yet throughout the grand reflections is the memory of 'Dear Child! dear Girl!,' the outburst of genuine feeling that is so much a part of Wordsworth's poetry.

Not all the sonnets are successful: some are plainly tedious, and others are mistakenly pretentious. The long series of *Ecclesiastical Sonnets*, written at the suggestion of Sir George Beaumont, has the air of a dull exercise. At their best, however, the sonnets have the same kind of forceful austerity that Wordsworth admired in Milton, and the characteristic blend of homely tenderness and lofty sentiment.

In the later sonnets something of the magic goes out of Wordsworth's poetry. It is difficult to say what it is, but the ideas that seemed so powerful now become commonplace. The same can be said of *The Excursion* (1814), with the exception of Book I, and that is better read in its earlier version as 'The Ruined Cottage' (written 1797–1798). There it is a moving story of the decline of a family and the ruin of their lives and hopes by sickness and economic recession (in some respects a return to the preoccupations of the Salisbury Plain poems). In *The Excursion* it is still very fine, though to some tastes the Christian conclusion is false and trite. The central figure of Margaret, the last human tenant of the ruined cottage (last human tenant as opposed to the natural creatures who later take up their abode there), is drawn, with a sustained economy and gravity: she is

> ... a Woman of a steady mind
> Tender and deep in her excess of love;   (I.513–514)

while her husband is 'Frugal affectionate, sober, and withal/ Keenly industrious.' A succession of calamities (bad harvests, war, and illness), however, causes him to lose his work and sense of purpose, and he finally leaves to join the army. Margaret has to part with her elder child to a kind farmer; the younger child dies; and she is left alone, waiting for the return that never comes. Her love and loyalty prevent her from leaving the cottage, and from having any other hope in life; her continued disappointment leads to her sickness and death.

Her story is told by a central figure in *The Excursion*, the Wanderer (in the earliest version, the Pedlar), who is one of those ideal Wordsworth characters who has given up a regular and settled employment for something that is freer and more haphazard. He has no interest in what Wordsworth called 'getting and spending'; he is a travelling and solitary man, who possesses a tranquil and steady mind. The result is that his energies are not directed to his own problems:

> ... and, by nature tuned
> And constant disposition of his thoughts
> To sympathy with man, he was alive
> To all that was enjoyed where'er he went,
> And all that was endured; for, in himself
> Happy, and quiet in his cheerfulness,
> He had no painful pressure from without
> That made him turn aside from wretchedness
> With coward fears. He could *afford* to suffer
> With those whom he saw suffer. ...

The Wanderer is an ideal figure, who is contrasted in the poem with the Solitary, a man who has experienced the hopes and miseries of the French Revolution, and whose personal sufferings have made him misanthropic. A third character, the Pastor, is perhaps the most important of all: he dominates the latter part of the poem with his practical Christian wisdom, and the final book ends with a delightful scene of the Pastor and his family. This forms an obvious contrast to the first book of the poem: from the ruined family to the happy and prosperous one is a journey that involves a full acceptance and understanding of human misery, together with an ability to remain optimistic and benevolent. Both the Wanderer, in his solitude and peripatetic life, and the Pastor, who stands for the settled family life, are able to bring comfort to others and remain at peace with themselves.

The Excursion is thus an extended illustration of different ways of approaching the central problems of human life – the failure of hopes, the loss of loved ones, the doubtful consolations of religion. In its counselling of orthodox Christian belief, *The Excursion* looks toward the work of the later Wordsworth, and indeed the poet's orthodoxy may be one reason why his later poetry is not informed by the same intense conviction as the earlier poetry that expresses his sense of natural power. It is this awareness of the power of natural life and its relation to the mind of man that Wordsworth conveys so well: it is a power beside which the preoccupation of man with material things seems idle, and it is a power whose essential optimism is a counterbalance to the very real suffering and misery of men. If men were to behave with this power as their guide, there would be less misery, for human unhappiness often comes from a failure of society to provide properly for its members. Instead, there would be

... a better time,
More wise desires, and simpler manners. ...   (103–104)

These lines come from the preface to *The Excursion*, originally part of a longer poem entitled 'Home at

60

Grasmere.' In it we see a summary of many of Wordsworth's most deeply held beliefs. As so often, Milton is in the background as Wordsworth thinks of the earthly paradise. He knows that he (like Milton visiting Hell) will have to travel

> ... near the tribes
> And fellowships of men, and see ill sights
> Of madding passions mutually inflamed;
> Must hear Humanity in fields and groves
> Pipe solitary anguish; or must hang
> Brooding above the fierce confederate storm
> Of sorrow, barricadoed evermore
> Within the walls of cities— ...
>
> (73–80)

But he also intends to celebrate the beauties of paradise, not just as a concept or an idea, but as an actual possibility:

> ... Paradise, and groves
> Elysian, Fortunate Fields—like those of old
> Sought in the Atlantic Main—why should they be
> A history only of departed things,
> Or a mere fiction of what never was?
> For the discerning intellect of Man,
> When wedded to this goodly universe
> In love and holy passion, shall find these
> A simple produce of the common day.
>
> (47–55)

The last beautiful line, with its utter simplicity (and the language really used by men), emphasizes the way in which Wordsworth regarded the universe that he found all around him. It was a world that contained its full share of human misery, but that had the power of being transformed by the human mind. In that process, the poet had his full part to play, and that is why Wordsworth always thought of himself as a teacher. The poet as he described him in the preface to *Lyrical Ballads* is many things, but above all

He is the rock of defence for human nature; an upholder and preserver, carrying everywhere with him relationship and love.
(*Poetical Works*, II.396)

WILLIAM WORDSWORTH

A Select Bibliography

(Place of publication London, unless stated otherwise)

Bibliography

A CONCORDANCE TO THE POEMS OF WILLIAM WORDSWORTH, by
L. Cooper (1911).

A BIBLIOGRAPHY OF THE WRITINGS IN PROSE AND VERSE OF
WILLIAM WORDSWORTH, T. J. Wise (1916).

TWO LAKE POETS: a catalogue of printed books, manuscripts
etc., by Wordsworth and Coleridge, by T. J. Wise (1927).

WORDSWORTHIAN CRITICISM: a guide and bibliography, by
J. V. Logan, Columbus, Ohio (1947).

CATALOGUE OF THE LIBRARY AT DOVE COTTAGE (1948).

THE CORNELL WORDSWORTH COLLECTION, G. H. Henley,
comp. (1957).

WORDSWORTHIAN CRITICISM 1945-1964: an annotated bibliography, by E. F. Henley and D. H. Stam, New York
(1965).

WORDSWORTHIAN CRITICISM 1964-1973: an annotated bibliography, including additions to Wordsworthian Criticism
1945-1964, by D. H. Stam, New York (1974).

Collected Works

POEMS, INCLUDING LYRICAL BALLADS, 2 vols., the first collected
ed., (1915).

MISCELLANEOUS POEMS, 4 vols. (1820-1827), 5 vols. (1832),
6 vols. (1836-1846), 7 vols. (1849-1850).

THE POEMS (1845).

THE POETICAL WORKS, 6 vols., with I. Fenwick's notes (1857).

THE POETICAL WORKS, ed. T. Hutchinson (1895), rev. by E. de
Selincourt (1950), the *Oxford Standard Authors* series,
also in *Oxford Paperback* (1969).

THE POETICAL WORKS, 5 vols., eds. E. de Selincourt and
H. Darbishire, Oxford (1940-1949, rev. ed. 1952-1959).

THE PROSE WORKS OF WILLIAM WORDSWORTH, 3 vols., eds.
W. J. B. Owen and J. W. Smyser, Oxford (1974).

WILLIAM WORDSWORTH: THE POEMS, 2 vols., ed. J. O. Hayden,
Harmondsworth (1977), does not include *The Prelude*.

THE CORNELL WORDSWORTH, ed. S. Parrish, Ithaca, N.Y.-
Hassocks, Sussex (1975–
THE SALISBURY PLAIN POEMS, ed. S. Gill (1975).
THE PRELUDE, 1798-99, ed. S. Parrish (1977).
HOME AT GRASMERE, ed. B. Darlington (1977).
THE RUINED COTTAGE AND THE PEDLAR, ed. J. Butler (1979).
BENJAMIN THE WAGGONER, ed. Paul F. Betz (1981).
THE BORDERERS, ed. Robert Osborn (1982).

Selected Works
POEMS OF WORDSWORTH, ed. M. Arnold (1879).
POEMS IN TWO VOLUMES, ed. T. Hutchinson (1897), from the
original ed. 1807, edited by H. Darbyshire (1914) and rev.
ed. (1952).
WORDSWORTH, SELECTED POETRY AND PROSE, ed. J. Butt
(1964).
WILLIAM WORDSWORTH: SELECTED POETRY AND PROSE, ed.
G. H. Hartman, New York (1969).
A CHOICE OF WORDSWORTH'S VERSE, ed. R. S. Thomas (1971).
WORDSWORTH'S LITERARY CRITICISM, ed. W. J. B. Owen
(1974).
WILLIAM WORDSWORTH: SELECTED POEMS, ed. W. Davies
(1975).

Separate Works
AN EVENING WALK, *Verse* (1793).
DESCRIPTIVE SKETCHES, *Verse* (1793).
LYRICAL BALLADS, WITH A FEW OTHER POEMS, Bristol (1798),
also in R. L. Brett and A. R. Jones, eds. (1965), W. J. B.
Owen ed. (1967) and Scolar Press facs. ed. (1971)..
LYRICAL BALLADS, WITH OTHER POEMS, 2 vols. (1800), also in D.
Roper, ed. *Lyrical Ballads*, 1805 (1968).
POEMS, IN TWO VOLUMES (1807), also in H. Darbishire, ed.
(1914).
CONCERNING THE RELATIONS OF GREAT BRITAIN, SPAIN, AND
PORTUGAL TO EACH OTHER, AND TO THE COMMON ENEMY AT
THIS CRISIS, AND SPECIFICALLY AS AFFECTED BY THE CONVEN-
TION OF CINTRA, *Prose* (1809).
THE EXCURSION, BEING A PORTION OF THE 'THE RECLUSE', *Verse*
(1814).
THE WHITE DOE OF RYLSTONE, verse (1815), also in Scolar
Press facs. ed. (1971).
THANKSGIVING ODE, 18 January 1816 (1816).

PETER BELL, A TALE IN VERSE (1819).

THE WAGGONER, *Verse* (1819).

THE RIVER DUDDON, A SERIES OF SONNETS (1820).

MEMORIALS OF A TOUR ON THE CONTINENT, *Verse* (1822).

ECCLESIASTICAL SKETCHES, *Verse* (1822).

A DESCRIPTION OF THE SCENERY OF THE LAKES IN THE NORTH OF ENGLAND: ORIGINALLY PUBLISHED WITH SELECT VIEWS IN CUMBERLAND, WESTMORLAND, ETC., BY THE REV. J. WILKINSON, *Prose* (1822).

YARROW REVISITED, AND OTHER POEMS (1835).

A GUIDE THROUGH THE DISTRICT OF THE LAKES IN THE NORTH OF ENGLAND, *Prose* (1835), also in E. de. Selincourt, ed. (1906).

THE SONNETS OF WILLIAM WORDSWORTH (1838).

POEMS CHIEFLY OF EARLY AND LATE YEARS: INCLUDING THE BORDERERS: A TRAGEDY (1842).

ODE ON THE THE INSTALLATION OF HIS ROYAL HIGHNESS PRINCE ALBERT AS CHANCELLOR OF THE UNIVERITY OF CAMBRIDGE (1847).

THE PRELUDE OR GROWTH OF A POET'S MIND: AN AUTO-BIOGRAPHICAL POEM (1850) – the standard ed. is that of E. de Selincourt, edited from the MSS with intro. and notes (1926), rev. by H. Darbishire, Oxford English Texts (1959); 1805 text E. de Selincourt, ed. rev. by S. Gill (1970); 1805 and 1850 texts, J. C. Maxwell, ed. Harmondsworth (1971); 1799, 1805 and 1850 texts, J. Wordsworth, M. H. Abrams and S. Gill, eds., New York (1979).

JOURNALS OF DOROTHY WORDSWORTH, 2 vols., ed. E. de Selincourt (1941), also M. Moorman, ed. (1971).

Letters

LETTERS OF THE WORDSWORTH FAMILY, 3 vols., ed. W. Knight (1907).

WORDSWORTH AND REED: THE POET'S CORRESPONDENCE WITH HIS AMERICAN EDITOR: 1836-50, ed. L. N. Broughton (1933).

LETTERS OF WILLIAM AND DOROTHY WORDSWORTH, 6 vols., ed. E. de Selincourt, Oxford (1935-39), rev. ed. in progress: *The Early Years, 1787-1805*, rev. by C. L. Shaver (1967), *The Middle Years, Part 1, 1806-1811*, rev. by M. Moorman (1969), *The Middle Years, Part 2, 1812-1820*, rev. by M. Moorman and A. G. Hill (1970), *The Later Years, Part 1*,

1821-1828, Part II, 1829-1834, Part III, 1835-1839, ed. by A. G. Hill (1978, 1979, 1982).

SOME LETTERS OF THE WORDSWORTH FAMILY, ed. L. N. Broughton, Ithaca, N.Y. (1942).

LETTERS OF WILLIAM WORDSWORTH, ed. P. Wayne (1954), in the World's Classics edition.

THE LETTERS OF MARY WORDSWORTH, 1800-1858, ed. M. E. Burton.

THE LETTERS OF JOHN WORDSWORTH, ed. C. H. Ketcham, Ithaca, N.Y. (1969)

Biographical and Critical Studies

BIOGRAPHIA LITERARIA, by S. T. Coleridge (1817), ed. J. Shawcross, Oxford (1907), also G. Watson, ed. (1971); the most valuable modern edition is by James Engell and W. Jackson Bate, *The Collected Works of Samuel Taylor Coleridge*, vol. 7 (1983).

LECTURES ON THE ENGLISH POETS, by W. Hazlitt (1918).

IMAGINARY CONVERSATIONS OF LITERARY MEN AND STATESMEN, Vol. 1, by W. S. Landor (1924).

THE SPIRIT OF THE AGE, by W. Hazlitt (1825).

"LITERARY AND LAKE REMINISCENCES", by T. De Quincey, in *Tait*'s magazine (1834, 1839) – see also COLLECTED WRITINGS OF DE QUINCEY, ed. D. Masson (1889-1890).

EARLY RECOLLECTIONS, by J. Cottle (1937).

MODERN PAINTERS, by J. Ruskin (1840-1860).

MEMOIRS OF WILLIAM WORDSWORTH, 2 vols. by C. Wordsworth (1851).

RECREATIONS OF CHRISTOPHER NORTH, vol. II, by J. Wilson (1854).

TRANSACTIONS OF THE WORDSWORTH SOCIETY, ed. W. Knight (1882-1887).

ESSAYS IN CRITICISM, 2nd ser., by M. Arnold (1888).

LITERARY ASSOCIATIONS OF THE LAKES, by H. D. Rawnsley (1894).

LA JEUNESSE DE WILLIAM WORDSWORTH, by E. Legouis, Paris (1896), trans. by J. W. Matthews as "The Early Life of William Wordsworth" (1897).

APPRECIATIONS, by W. Pater (1899).

WORDSWORTH, by W. Raleigh (1903).

ENGLISH POETRY AND GERMAN PHILOSOPHY IN THE AGE OF WORDSWORTH, by A. C. Bradley (1909).

OXFORD LECTURES ON POETRY, by A. C. Bradley (1909).

BLAKE, COLERIDGE, WORDSWORTH, ETC: SELECTIONS FROM THE REMAINS OF HENRY CRABB ROBINSON, ed. E. J. Morley (1922).

WILLIAM WORDSWORTH AND ANNETTE VALLON, by E. Legouis (1922).

WORDSWORTH: LECTURES AND ESSAYS, by H. W. Garrod (1923).

WORDSWORTH, by H. Reed (1930), rev. ed. (1948).

DOROTHY WORDSWORTH: A BIOGRAPHY, by E. de Selincourt (1933).

WORDSWORTH, by P. Burra (1936).

WORDSWORTH AND COLERIDGE: STUDIES IN HONOUR OF GEORGE McLEAN HARPER, ed. E. L. Griggs, Princeton, N.J. (1939).

LESLIE STEPHEN AND MATTHEW ARNOLD AS CRITICS OF WORDSWORTH, by J. D. Wilson (1939).

WORDSWORTH'S FORMATIVE YEARS, by G. W. Meyer, Ann Arbor, Mich. (1943).

A STUDY OF WORDSWORTH, by J. C. Smith (1944).

STRANGE SEAS OF THOUGHT: STUDIES IN WORDSWORTH'S PHILOSOPHY OF MAN AND NATURE, by N. P. Stallknecht, Durham, N.C. (1945).

WORDSWORTHIAN AND OTHER STUDIES, by E. de Selincourt (1947).

WORDSWORTH: AN INTRODUCTION AND A SELECTION, by N. Nicholson (1949).

THE POET WORDSWORTH by H. Darbishire (1950).
—Clark Lectures (1949) Oxford Paperback (1966).

WORDSWORTH AT CAMBRIDGE: A RECORD OF THE COMMEMORATION HELD AT ST. JOHN'S COLLEGE, CAMBRIDGE (1950).
—contains a detailed survey of Wordsworth portraits.

WORDSWORTH: CENTENARY STUDIES, ed. G. T. Dunklin, Princeton, N.J. (1950).

THE ART OF WORDSWORTH, by L. Abercrombie (1952).

WORDSWORTH AND COLERIDGE, by H. M. Margoliouth (1953).

THE EGOTISTICAL SUBLIME: A HISTORY OF WORDSWORTH'S IMAGINATION, by J. Jones (1954).

WORDSWORTH: A RE-INTERPRETATION, by F. W. Bateson (1954); rev. ed. (1956).

WILLIAM WORDSWORTH: A BIOGRAPHY, 2 vols. by M. Moorman, Oxford (1957-65), reprinted in Oxford Paperback (1968).

WORDSWORTH'S CAMBRIDGE EDUCATION, by B. R. Schneider (1957).

THE NOTEBOOKS OF SAMUEL TAYLOR COLERIDGE, 2 vols., ed. K. Coburn (1957).

POLITICS AND THE POET: A STUDY OF WORDSWORTH, by F. M. Todd (1957).

THE EARLY WORDSWORTHIAN MILIEU, ed. Z. S. Fink (1958). —a notebook of Christopher Wordsworth, with a few entries by William Wordsworth.

THE LIMITS OF MORTALITY: AN ESSAY ON WORDSWORTH'S MAJOR POEMS, by D. Ferry, Middleton, Conn. (1959).

PORTRAITS OF WORDSWORTH, by F. Blanshard (1959).

THE SIMPLE WORDSWORTH: STUDIES IN THE POEMS, 1797-1807, by J. F. Danby (1960).

ROMANTIC PARADOX: AN ESSAY ON THE POETRY OF WORDS-WORTH, by C. C. Clarke (1963).

ON WORDSWORTH'S PRELUDE, by H. Lindenberger (1963).

WILLIAM WORDSWORTH: THE PRELUDE AND OTHER POEMS, by J. F. Danby (1963).

WORDSWORTH AND THE POETRY OF SINCERITY, by D. Perkins, Cambridge, Mass. (1964).

WORDSWORTH'S POETRY 1787-1814, by G. H. Hartman, New Haven, Conn. (1964), contains a good critical bibliography.

WORDSWORTH AND THE ARTIST'S VISION, by A. King (1966).

THE LANDSCAPE OF MEMORY, by C. Salvesen (1966).

THE UNITY OF WORDSWORTH'S POETRY, by G. B. Groom (1966).

WORDSWORTH: THE CHRONOLOGY OF THE EARLY YEARS 1770-1779, by M. L. Reed, London-Cambridge, Mass. (1967).

WORDSWORTH: A PHILOSOPHICAL APPROACH, by M. Rader, Oxford (1967).

WORDSWORTH AND HIS WORLD, by F. E. Halliday (1969), with 140 illustrations.

WILLIAM WORDSWORTH, by G. Durrant (1969), Cambridge British Authors paperback.

WORDSWORTH, by C. Woodring, Cambridge, Mass. (1968).

THE MUSIC OF HUMANITY: A CRITICAL STUDY OF WORDSWORTH'S "RUINED COTTAGE" INCORPORATING TEXTS FROM A MANU-SCRIPT of 1799-1800, by C. Woodring (1969).

WORDSWORTH'S THEORY OF POETRY: THE TRANSFORMING IMAGINATION, by J. A. W. Heffernan, Ithaca, N.Y. (1969).

WILLIAM WORDSWORTH: 1770-1969, by J. Wordsworth (1969), British Academy Chatterton Lecture..

WORDSWORTH AND THE ADEQUACY OF LANDSCAPE, by D. Wesling (1970).

WORDSWORTH AND THE GREAT SYSTEM, by G. Durrant (1970).

PICTURESQUE LANDSCAPE AND ENGLISH ROMANTIC POETRY, by J. R. Watson (1970).

WORDSWORTH AND COLERIDGE IN THEIR TIME, by A. S. Byatt (1970).

WORDSWORTH AND COLERIDGE, by W. Heath, Oxford (1970).

COLERIDGE AND WORDSWORTH: THE POETRY OF GROWTH, by S. Prickett, Cambridge (1970).

BICENTENARY WORDSWORTH STUDIES IN MEMORY OF JOHN ALBAN FINCH, ed. J. Wordsworth, Ithaca, N.Y. (1971).

WORDSWORTH AND THE POETRY OF ENCOUNTER, by F. Garber, Urbana, Ill. (1971).

WORDSWORTH'S DIRGE AND PROMISE, by G. K. Thomas, Lincoln, Nebr. (1971).

WORDSWORTH'S EXPERIMENTS WITH TRADITION, by J. R. Curtis, Ithaca, N.Y. (1971).

WILLIAM WORDSWORTH, by R. Noyes, New York (1971).

THE CHARACTER OF THE POET, by R. J. Onorato, Princeton, N.J. (1971).

WILLIAM WORDSWORTH, ed. G. McMaster, Harmondsworth (1972), Penguin Critical Anthology.

WORDSWORTH, LYRICAL BALLADS, eds. A. R. Jones and W. Tydeman (1972), a casebook.

WORDSWORTH, THE PRELUDE: A Casebook, eds. W. J. Harvey and R. Gravil (1972).

THE FIGURE IN A LANDSCAPE: WORDSWORTH'S EARLY POETRY, by R. Sharrock (1972), British Academy Warton Lecture.

THE ART OF THE LYRICAL BALLADS, by S. M. Parish, Cambridge, Mass. (1973).

THE MAKING OF WORDSWORTH'S POETRY, by P. D. Sheats, Cambridge, Mass. (1973).

THE PHILOSOPHIC MIND, by A. Grob, Columbus, Ohio (1973).

WORDSWORTH AND THE SUBLIME, by A. O. Wlecke, Berkeley (1973).

WORDSWORTH, A COLLECTION OF CRITICAL ESSAYS, ed. M. H. Abrams, Englewood Cliffs, N.J. (1973).

WORDSWORTH AND THE SONNET, by L. M. Johnson, Copenhagen (1973).

THE CONFESSIONAL IMAGINATION, by F. D. McConnell, Baltimore (1974).

WORDSWORTH: THE CHRONOLOGY OF THE MIDDLE YEARS, 1800–1815, by M. L. Reed, Cambridge, Mass. (1975).

WORDSWORTH'S "NATURAL METHODISM", by R. E. Brantley, New Haven, Conn. (1975).

ALL SHADES OF CONSCIOUSNESS: WORDSWORTH'S POETRY AND THE SELF IN TIME, by E. L. Stelzig, The Hague (1975).

WORDSWORTH AND COLERIDGE: THE LYRICAL BALLADS, by S. Prickett (1975).

TRADITION AND EXPERIMENT IN WORDSWORTH'S LYRICAL BALLADS (1978) by M. Jacobus, Oxford (1976).

WHY THE LYRICAL BALLADS?, by J. E. Jordan, Berkeley (1976).

WORDSWORTH: LANGUAGE AS COUNTER-SPIRIT, by F. Ferguson, New Haven, Conn. (1977).

WORDSWORTH AND THE HUMAN HEART, by J. Beer (1977).

WORDSWORTH IN TIME, by J. B. Beer (1979).

THE MAKINGS OF A MUSIC: REFLECTIONS ON THE POETRY OF WORDSWORTH AND YEATS, by Seamus Heaney, Liverpool (1980).

WORDSWORTH AND THE POETRY OF HUMAN SUFFERING, by J. H. Averill, Ithaca (1980).

WORDSWORTH'S PHILOSOPHICAL POETRY, by J. A. Hodgson, Lincoln, Nebr. (1980).

WORDSWORTH'S POETRY OF THE IMAGINATION, by N. Sherry (1980).

WORDSWORTH, by A. Adams, Edinburgh (1981).

WORDSWORTH AND THE BEGINNING OF MODERN POETRY, by R. Rehder (1981).

WILLIAM WORDSWORTH: THE POETRY OF GRANDEUR AND TENDERNESS, by D. Pirie (1982).

WORDSWORTH AND THE FIGURINGS OF THE REAL, by David Simpson (1982).

WORDSWORTH'S VITAL SOUL, by J. R. Watson (1982).

WILLIAM WORDSWORTH: THE BORDERS OF VISION, by Jonathan Wordsworth (1983).

Printed and bound by CPI Group (UK) Ltd, Croydon, CR0 4YY

13/04/2025

14656596-0001